4th Workshop on Inquisitiveness Below and Beyond the Sentence Boundary (InqBnB4)

Nancy, France
20 June 2023

ISBN: 978-1-7138-9053-9

Printed from e-media with permission by:

Curran Associates, Inc.
57 Morehouse Lane
Red Hook, NY 12571

Some format issues inherent in the e-media version may also appear in this print version.

Printed with permission by Curran Associates, Inc. (2025)

For permission requests, please contact the Association for Computational Linguistics
at the address below.

Association for Computational Linguistics
209 N. Eighth Street
Stroudsburg, Pennsylvania 18360

Phone: 1-570-476-8006
Fax: 1-570-476-0860

acl@aclweb.org

Additional copies of this publication are available from:

Curran Associates, Inc.
57 Morehouse Lane
Red Hook, NY 12571 USA
Phone: 845-758-0400
Fax: 845-758-2633
Email: curran@proceedings.com
Web: www.proceedings.com

InqBnB4

The 4th Workshop on Inquisitiveness Below and Beyond the Sentence Boundary

Proceedings of the Workshop

June 20, 2023
Nancy, France

(hosted by IWCS 2023, SIGSEM)

Order copies of this and other ACL proceedings from:

Association for Computational Linguistics (ACL)
209 N. Eighth Street
Stroudsburg, PA 18360
USA
Tel: +1-570-476-8006
Fax: +1-570-476-0860
acl@aclweb.org

Preface

This volume contains the 6 papers accepted and presented at the fourth edition of the workshop Inquisitiveness Below and Beyond the Sentence Boundary (InqBnB4). It was held in Nancy (France) on 20th June 2023, with the 15th International Conference on Computational Semantic (IWCS 2023).

`https://iwcs2023.loria.fr/inqbnb4-inquisitiveness-below-and-beyond-the-sentence-boundary/`

InqBnB is a workshop series bringing together researchers interested in the semantics and pragmatics of interrogatives. This series was originally organized by the Inquisitive Semantics Group of the Institute for Logic, Language and Computation (ILLC) from the University of Amsterdam. As such, the focus point mainly revolves around analyses using or related to inquisitive semantics. These interactions stimulated the creation of a small community around this topic.

The first edition was held in June 2017 in Broek in Waterland, close to Amsterdam, the Netherlands. It featured 20 invited speakers. The second edition was held in December 2017 in Amsterdam. Among 25 submitted papers, 11 were accepted, and 6 speakers were additionally invited. The third edition was held in June 2019, again in Amsterdam. It featured 20 invited speakers.

With InqBnB4, we aimed at bringing this community outside of its initial zone. First, by adjoining this workshop to a larger and international conference. Second, by changing the location and organizer affiliations. By doing so, we hoped to expose this research field to a wider audience, and at the same time we hoped to see more diversity in submitted study approaches.

InqBnB4 invited submissions on original and unpublished research focused on the properties of inquisitive content. We were mainly interested in theoretical questions, formal models and empirical works.

Below the sentence boundary:

- Which operators (connectives, quantifiers, modals, conditionals) generate inquisitiveness?
- How do these operators project the inquisitive content of their arguments?
- How does inquisitive content interact with informative content in compositional semantics?

Beyond the sentence boundary:

- How do conventions of use interact with inquisitive content?
- In which ways is pragmatics sensitive to inquisitive content?
- What kind of discourse anaphora are licensed by inquisitive expressions?

We thank everyone who submitted papers. We also thank everyone who accepted to be part of the program committee. The meeting was enriched by the inspirational talks from Wataru Uegaki and Todor Koev.

We are thankful to the NWO VICI grant "QuSign: Questions in sign language" (2021-2026) for financing invited speaker fees. We also thank the LORIA for hosting the website and the IDMC (Institut des Sciences du Digital, Management et Cognition) at Pôle Herbert Simon, the venue of the workshop. Finally, this workshop wouldn't have been possible without the help of IWCS 2023. We are very grateful to Maxime Amblard and Ellen Breitholtz, all the organizers and the sponsors of IWCS 2023 (CNRS, Inria, Université de Lorraine, University of Gothenburg, Erdil and Métropole du Grand Nancy).

Valentin D. Richard and Floris Roelofsen

Organizing Committee

Valentin D. Richard, Loria, Université de Lorraine, Nancy, France

Philippe de Groote, Loria, INRIA Nancy – Grand Est, Nancy, France

Floris Roelofsen, ILLC, Universiteit van Amsterdam, Amsterdam, The Netherlands

Programme Committee

Local Chair: Valentin D. Richard, Université de Lorraine

Chair: Floris Roelofsen, ILLC, Universiteit van Amsterdam

Maria Aloni, Universiteit van Amsterdam

Lucas Champollion, New York University (NYU)

Jakub Dotlačil, Universiteit Utrecht

Jonathan Ginzburg, Université Paris Cité

Philippe de Groote, INRIA Nancy – Grand Est

Todor Koev, Universität Konstanz

Reinhard Muskens, Universiteit van Amsterdam

Maribel Romero, Universität Konstanz

Wataru Uegaki, University of Edinburgh

Yimei Xiang, Rutgers Linguistics

Invited Speakers

Todor Koev, Universität Konstanz

Wataru Uegaki, University of Edinburgh

Table of Contents

Program of InqBnB4

9:00–9:30 Welcoming

9:30–9:40 Introducing words

9:40–10:35 Invited talk: *The MECORE database and the *whether-puzzle*
Wataru Uegaki

10:35–11:00 ***break***

11:00–12:30 **First session:**

Short answers as tests: A post-suppositional view on wh-questions and answers
Linmin Zhang

Referential Transparency and Inquisitiveness
Jonathan Ginzburg and Andy Lücking

Uninquisitive questions
Tom Roberts

Lunch
12:30–14:00

14:00–15:30 **Second session:**

mage as a bias particle in interrogatives
Maryam Mohammadi

Dynamic Questions: Evidence from Mandarin Think–"Xiang"
Anshun Zheng

The indefinite-interrogative affinity in sign languages: the case of Catalan Sign Language
Raquel Veiga Busto, Floris Roelofsen and Alexandra Navarrete González

15:30–16:00 ***break***

16:00–16:55 Invited talk: *Question Bias, Polarity Focus, and Salience*
Todor Koev (joint work with Cory Bill)

16:55–17:00 Final words

Short answers as tests: A post-suppositional view on *wh*-questions and answers

Linmin Zhang
NYU Shanghai, 567 West Yangsi Road, Shanghai, 200126, China
linmin.zhang@nyu.edu, zhanglinmin@gmail.com

Abstract

This paper explores a post-suppositional view on *wh*-questions and their answers with dynamic semantics. Inspired by Brasoveanu (2013); Charlow (2017); Bumford (2017), I propose a unified treatment of items like modified numerals, focus items, and *wh*-items: they (i) introduce a discourse referent (dref) in a non-deterministic way and (ii) impose definiteness tests (and additional tests) in a delayed, post-suppositional manner at the sentential / discourse level. Thus, with a question like *who smiled*, the (maximally informative) dref 'the one(s) who smiled' is derived. A short answer like '*Mary and Max*' is considered another post-supposition-like, delayed test, checking whether the dref 'the one(s) who smiled' is identical to (or includes) the sum **Mary⊕Max**. I analyze various question-related phenomena to see how far this proposal can go.

1 Introduction

This paper explores a post-suppositional perspective on the semantics of *wh*-questions and (short) answers within a dynamic semantics framework.

In this introduction, I present the conceptual and technical motivations behind this project.

For a *wh*-question like (1), it is easy to see that the short answer in (1a) is guaranteed to be a complete true answer, and the corresponding propositional answer is actually tautological. However, despite its being true and complete, interlocutors usually don't accept such an answer, because it is derivable from the question and provides no new information. In contrast, (1b) illustrates what a typical acceptable short answer should look like.

(1) Who smiled?

a. The one(s) who smiled. **Short Ans.**
$\rightsquigarrow$ The one(s) who smiled smiled.

b. Mary and Max. **Short Ans.**
$\rightsquigarrow$ Mary and Max smiled.

The above observation suggests that a good short answer to a *wh*-question provides new information about **something definite** that has already been established and restricted by the *wh*-question.

This observation is reminiscent of existing literature on **post-suppositional** phenomena, i.e., delayed tests that (i) check definiteness or (ii) provide additional information about something definite.

Brasoveanu (2013) provides a post-supposition-based account for modified numerals in cumulative-reading sentences.[1]

(2) Exactly 3^u boys saw exactly 5^ν movies.
Cumulative reading of (2):

$$\underbrace{\sigma x \sigma y[\text{BOY}(x) \wedge \text{MOVIE}(y) \wedge \text{SEE}(x,y)]}_{\text{the mereologically maximal } x \text{ and } y \text{ satisfying these restrictions}}$$
$$\underbrace{\wedge\, |y| = 5 \wedge |x| = 3}_{\text{cardinality tests}}$$

(σ: maximality operator; for notation simplicity, cumulative closure is assumed.)

As sketched out in (2), the semantic contribution of modified numerals (i.e., the underlined parts) includes several layers:

First, modified numerals introduce, in a non-deterministic way, (potentially plural) discourse referents (drefs), x and y (assigned to u and ν respectively).

Second, after various relevant restrictions are added onto these drefs (here $\text{BOY}(x)$, $\text{MOVIE}(y)$, and $\text{SEE}(x, y)$), modified numerals further contribute maximality tests and cardinality tests. Specifically, (i) the maximality operators σ pick out the mereologically maximal x and y, i.e., x that is equal to the sum of all boys who saw any movies, and y that is equal to the sum of all movies seen by any boys; (ii) these mereologically maximal drefs are finally checked for their cardinality.

[1] Sentence (2) also has a distributive reading, which is not discussed in this paper (see also Brasoveanu 2013).

Proceedings of the 4th Workshop on Inquisitiveness Below and Beyond the Sentence Boundary (InqBnB4), pages 1–10

Therefore, eventually, (2) addresses the cardinality of all the boys who saw any movies (which is 3) and the cardinality of all the movies seen by any boys (which is 5).

Conceptually, cumulative-reading sentences and *wh*-questions are parallel in at least two aspects, which motivate a similar underlying analysis:

1. **Relativized definiteness**: The meaning of cumulative-reading sentence (2) is about all the boys who saw movies and all the movies seen by boys, not all the boys or all the movies in context. For *wh*-question (1), evidently, the sentence is about all those who smiled, not all people in context. In both cases, definiteness is relativized by information beyond the immediate DP.

2. **Additional information about relativized definite items**: Cardinalities in sentence (2) bring additional information about the boys who saw movies and the movies seen by boys. The good short answer in (1b) also provides additional information with regard to all those who smiled. The lack of this kind of additional information would often result in triviality and thus degradedness (see (1a) and (3)).

(3) ??The boys saw the movies.
Intended: 'The boys who saw movies saw the movies seen by boys.'

Under the analysis of (2) by Brasoveanu (2013), relativized definiteness is realized via a global application of maximality operators. Essentially, the derivation starts with non-deterministic alternatives. Then, crucially, definiteness tests are not applied immediately at the local DP level, but as post-suppositions, delayed to a higher, sentential level, resulting in relativized definiteness. Thus a pseudo-wide-scope effect in interpreting modified numerals is achieved, via splitting their semantic contribution into an indefinite part and a definite part.

Technically, the spirit of this post-suppositional (or split) analysis of Brasoveanu (2013) can be realized in different ways: e.g., higher-order dynamic generalized quantifiers, update semantics, post-suppositions (see Charlow 2017 for a detailed discussion and comparison). To facilitate presentation, here I adopt the dynamic semantics formalism of Bumford (2017), which is based on the non-deterministic state monad developed by Charlow (2014). A re-engineering of (2) is shown in (4).

(4) Exactly 3^u boys saw exactly 5^ν movies.

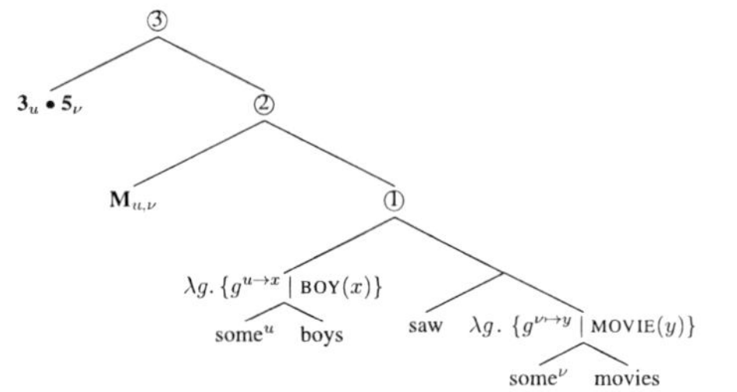

①: Introducing drefs and restrictions:
① $= [\![\text{some}^u \text{ boys saw some}^\nu \text{ movies}]\!] =$
$\lambda g.\,\left\{g^{u\mapsto x, \nu\mapsto y} \mid \text{MOVIE}(y), \text{BOY}(x), \text{SAW}(x,y)\right\}$

②: Applying maximality tests:
② $= \mathbf{M}_{u,\nu}(①) =$
$\lambda g.\,\{g^{u\mapsto x, \nu\mapsto y} \mid x = \Sigma x[\text{BOY}(x) \wedge \text{SEE}(x,y)],$
$y = \Sigma y[\text{MOVIE}(y) \wedge \text{SAW}(x,y)]\}$

③: Checking cardinalities:
③ $= \mathbf{3}_u \bullet \mathbf{5}_\nu(②)$
$=$ ②, if $|x| = 3$ and $|y| = 5$

(5) **Mereology-based maximality test:**
$\mathbf{M}_u \overset{\text{def}}{=} \lambda m.\lambda g.$
$\{h \in m(g) \mid \neg\exists h' \in m(g).\, h(u) \sqsubset h'(u)\}$

(6) **Cardinality test:**
$\mathbf{3}_u \overset{\text{def}}{=} \lambda m.\lambda g.\, m(g)$, if $|g(u)| = 3$
(if not, this returns $\emptyset$)

Within this framework, as illustrated in (2), meaning derivation is a series of updates from one information state to another, and an information state m (of type $g \to \{g\}$) is considered a function from an input assignment function to an output set of assignment functions. An update is true if the output set of assignment functions is not an empty set; an update is false if the output set of assignment functions is an empty set.

In (4), drefs are first introduced and various restrictions are added onto them (see ①). Maximality operators (see (5)) pick out the mereologically maximal drefs satisfying the restrictions (see ②). Finally, cardinality tests (see (6)) check the cardinalities of the maximal drefs (see ③). The cumulative-reading of (2) is true if the derivation does not return an empty set.

The rest of the paper is organized as follows. Section 2 presents the main proposal with this dynamic semantics formalism à la Bumford (2017). Section 3 explores further extensions of the proposal, analyzing various empirical phenomena hotly discussed in the existing literature on question semantics. Section 4 briefly compares the current work with recent related works. Section 5 concludes.

2 Proposal: *Wh*-questions and answers

(7) and (8) illustrate the core idea of the current proposal with a dynamic semantics implementation à la Bumford (2017).

(7) Who^u smiled? **wh-question**

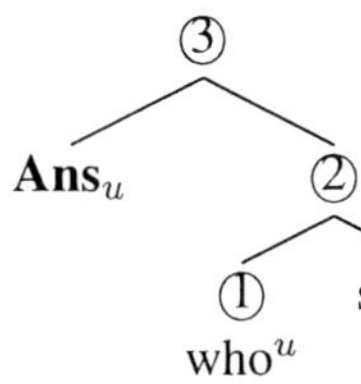

①: Introducing drefs:
① = ⟦who^u⟧ = ⟦some^u (people)⟧
$= \lambda g.\ \{g^{u \mapsto x} |\ \text{HUMAN}(x)\}$
②: More restrictions are added:
② = ⟦who^u smiled⟧
= ⟦some^u (people) smiled⟧
$= \lambda g.\ \{g^{u \mapsto x} |\ \text{HMN}(x) \wedge \text{SML}(x)\}$
③: Applying maximality tests:
③ = **Ans**$_u$(②) =
$\lambda g.\ \{g^{u \mapsto x} |\ x = \Sigma x[\text{HMN}(x) \wedge \text{SML}(x)]\}$

(8) Mary and Max **short answer to (7)**

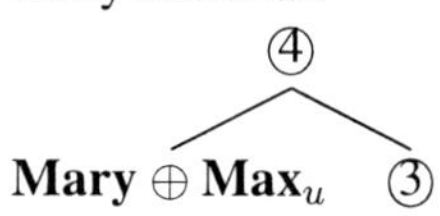

④: Checking additional information
④ = **Mary** ⊕ **Max**$_u$(③) =
$\lambda g.\ \{g^{u \mapsto x} |\ x = \Sigma x[\text{HMN}(x) \wedge \text{SML}(x)]\}$,
if $x =$ **Mary**⊕**Max** (or $x \sqsupseteq$ **Mary**⊕**Max**)

(9) **Maximality test** (informativeness-based):
Ans$_u \overset{\text{def}}{=} \lambda m.\lambda g.\ \{h \in m(g) \mid \neg\exists h' \in m(g).\ G(h(u)) <_{\text{info}} G(h'(u))\}$
(G is a context-dependent measurement function of informativeness.)[2]

a. Mereological maximality as a special case: **Ans**$_u \overset{\text{def}}{=} \lambda m.\lambda g.\ \{h \in m(g) \mid \neg\exists h' \in m(g).\ h(u) \sqsubset h'(u)\}$

(10) **Good short answer as another test**:

a. As a complete answer:
Mary ⊕ **Max**$_u \overset{\text{def}}{=}$
$\lambda m.\lambda g.\ m(g)$, if $g(u) =$ **My** ⊕ **Mx**
(if not, this returns $\emptyset$)

b. As a potentially partial answer:
Mary ⊕ **Max**$_u \overset{\text{def}}{=}$
$\lambda m.\lambda g.\ m(g)$, if $g(u) \sqsupseteq$ **My** ⊕ **Mx**
(if not, this returns $\emptyset$)

[2]See further discussion below on degree questions (Section 2.5). See also Zhang (2023a) for more discussion on maximal informativeness.

In (7), *who^u* first works like an indefinite and introduces a dref in a non-deterministic way. Given that the domain of this *wh*-item, *who*, is typically a set of human individuals, I also include the restriction HUMAN(x) here (see ① in (7)).

After other relevant restrictions are added (here SMILE(x), see ② in (7)), an operator **Ans**$_u$ is applied to ② (see (9) and ③ in (7)), picking out the definite dref that eventually leads to the maximally informative true answer to the *wh*-question.

Obviously, in this specific example (7), where the domain of the *wh*-item is a set of individuals and the predicate *smile* is inherently distributive, **Ans**$_u$ amounts to picking out the mereologically maximal dref, as shown in (9a). Essentially, ② means 'someone that smiled (smiled)', and ③ means 'the one(s) who smiled (smiled)'. In some sense, the question meaning (i.e., here ③ in (7)) is equivalent to the meaning of its analytical answer – ③.

(8) illustrates how a good short answer works. As defined in (10), **Mary** ⊕ **Max**$_u$ plays the same role as cardinality tests do in a cumulative-reading sentence (see (6) and (4)). If **Mary** ⊕ **Max**$_u$ is a complete answer, this test checks whether the maximal dref in ③ is identical to the sum **Mary** ⊕ **Max**$_u$. If **Mary** ⊕ **Max**$_u$ is a potentially partial answer, this test checks whether the sum **Mary** ⊕ **Max**$_u$ is part of the maximal dref in ③.

Basically, the above analysis shows (i) a compositional derivation of the meaning of a *wh*-question, (ii) the derivation of its (analytically) maximally informative true answer, and (iii) how a good short answer contributes information in addressing the *wh*-question. This analysis inherits many existing insights on question meanings.

2.1 Cross-sentential anaphora

Wh-items are parallel to indefinites in introducing drefs and supporting cross-sentential anaphora, as illustrated in (11) (see e.g., Comorovski 2013).

(11) a. Someone^u laughed. They$_u$ are noisy.
b. Who^u laughed? They$_u$ are noisy.

(12) a. $\lambda g.\ \{g^{u \mapsto x} |\ x = \Sigma x[\text{HMN}(x) \wedge \text{LG}(x)]\}$
b. $\lambda g.\ \{g^{u \mapsto x} |\ \text{NOISY}(x)\}$

The analysis of the first and second sentence in discourse (11b) is sketched in (12). The parallelism between *wh*-items and indefinites are immediately explained: both introduce drefs that support cross-sentential anaphora. The only difference is that a *wh*-item also involves (relativized) definiteness.

2.2 Short answers and the categorial approach

According to the categorial approach to *wh*-questions (Hausser and Zaefferer 1978), a *wh*-question denotes a function, which, when applying to its short answer, generates a (potentially complete true) propositional answer (see (13)).

(13) **Categorial approach**:
$[\![\text{who smiled}]\!] = \lambda x.\text{SMILE}(x)$

a. **Short answer**: Mary and Max

b. **Propositional answer**:
$[\text{Mary and Max}]_F$ smiled.

Similar to the categorial approach, the current analysis also composes a short answer with question meaning to derive the meaning of the corresponding propositional answer. As shown in (14), when the short answer $\mathbf{Mary} \oplus \mathbf{Max}_u$ (see (10)) is applied to the question meaning (see ③ in (7)), the meaning of the propositional answer (13b) is naturally derived (see also ④ in (8)).

(14)

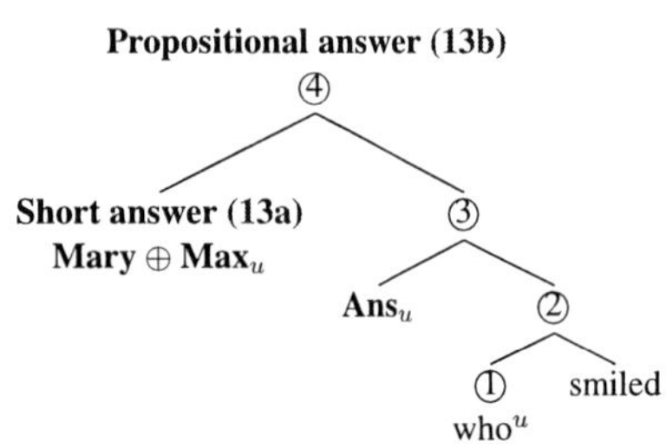

Thus under both the current analysis and the categorial approach, short answers are not derived from propositional analysis via ellipsis.

Jacobson (2016) also argues for the view that a short answers should not contain hidden, elided linguistic materials that would be part of a corresponding propositional answer. Actually Jacobson (2016) points out that for a *wh*-question like (7), a short answer like (8) is a genuine **answer** that addresses the *wh*-question, while a corresponding propositional answer is a derived **reply**. What a genuine answer really is is actually also reflected by the focus of a propositional answer.

The current analysis for short answers is in line with Jacobson (2016). A short answer as analyzed in (10) does not contain any ellipsis, and it only indicates (i) which dref in the *wh*-question the information $\mathbf{Mary} \oplus \mathbf{Max}_u$ is connected with and (ii) whether this connection is an identity relation or a part-whole relation. Sometimes the distinction between a complete and a potentially partial short answer can be reflected by intonation.

There are two major differences between the current analysis and the categorial approach. First, the current analysis addresses the definiteness in interpreting a *wh*-question. Second, under the current analysis, a good short answer actually behaves as if it takes a pseudo-wide-scope over the *wh*-question.

The current analysis also overcomes a few issues that challenge the original categorial approach.

As pointed out by Xiang (2021), under the traditional categorial approach, a *wh*-item is considered a λ-operator, thus this analysis fails to show the parallelism between *wh*-items and indefinites, which is widely observed cross-linguistically. Under the current analysis, *wh*-items are analyzed in exactly the same way as indefinites (see Section 2.1).

Xiang (2021) points out that the traditional categorial approach also faces the issues of (i) composing multi-*wh*-questions and (ii) question coordination. Section 3 will show how the above analysis can be extended to handle these issues.

2.3 Karttunen (1977): A *wh*-question means its complete true answer

The current analysis of *wh*-questions is also in the same spirit as Karttunen (1977): A *wh*-question has the same meaning as its complete true answer. This can be seen from ③ in (7).

According to Dayal (1996)'s Maximal Informativity Presupposition, a question presupposes the existence of a maximally informative true answer. Thus as far as a *wh*-question meets this requirement, the operator $\mathbf{Ans}_u$ (see (9)) is applicable to something like ② in (7), and ③ is derivable, which corresponds to the complete true answer. In other words, semantically, a *wh*-question is guaranteed to have an analytical complete true answer.

Different from Karttunen (1977), Hamblin (1973) analyzes the meaning of a *wh*-question as its possible propositional answers, instead of true propositional answers. Dependency data like (15) seem to support Hamblin (1973)'s view (see Dayal 2016), because according to our intuition, for (15), the interpretation of *where is Mary* seems a Hamblin set, i.e., a set of possible answers that address where Mary is. For this kind of dependency data, I'll account for them in Section 3.4 while maintaining a view in line with Karttunen (1977).

(15) What does John think? Where is Mary?
$\rightsquigarrow$ Where does John think Mary is?
(see, e.g., Dayal 2016)

2.4 The parallelism between *wh*-questions and *wh*-free-relatives

The current analysis also explains the parallelism between *wh*-questions and *wh*-free-relatives (see Caponigro 2003, 2004; Chierchia and Caponigro 2013). Essentially, a *wh*-free-relative can be considered the analytically true, definite, complete short answer to its corresponding *wh*-question.

As illustrated in (16), *wh*-free-relatives can be replaced by a definite DP, and (16a) and (16b) have the same truth condition. The analysis in (17) explains this truth-conditional equivalence. In (17), $\mathbf{Ans}_u$ plays the same role as a mereological maximality operator, leading to the maximal sum of things cooked by Adam (see (9a)).

(16) a. Jie tasted <u>what^u Adam cooked</u>. (from Caponigro 2004)
b. Jie tasted <u>the^u things Adam cooked</u>.

(17) $[\![\text{what}^u \text{ Adam cooked}]\!]$
$= \mathbf{Ans}_u(\lambda g.\ \{g^{u\mapsto x} | \textsc{cook}(\text{Adam}, x)\})$
$= \lambda g.\ \{g^{u\mapsto x} |\ x = \Sigma x[\textsc{cook}(\text{Adam}, x)]\}$
$= [\![\text{the}^u \text{ things Adam cooked}]\!]$

A further issue is about mention-some questions.

(18) Who^u can help her?

(19) Mary was looking for who^u can help her.
= Mary was looking for <u>someone^u</u> that can help her.
≠ Mary was looking for <u>all the^u people</u> that can help her.

As illustrated in (18) and (19), in these examples, there is also a parallelism between mention-some *wh*-questions (see (18)) and mentions-some *wh*-free-relatives (see (19)). However, it seems that mereological maximality is not involved.

Actually, in (9), I consider $\mathbf{Ans}_u$ a maximality operator that leads to the most informative answer. Maximal informativeness is not necessarily based on mereological maximality (see Zhang 2023a).

Thus for mention-some *wh*-questions and *wh*-free-relatives, the specific implementation of $\mathbf{Ans}_u$ should be different from the mereology-based one defined in (9a). Presumably, the application of $\mathbf{Ans}_u$ should involve (i) a context-relevant measurement of informativeness that takes into consideration the accessibility or availability of resources and/or (ii) some free-choice operator. I leave a detailed development of this idea for future research.

2.5 The parallelism between *wh*-questions and concealed questions

The current analysis also naturally captures the parallelism between *wh*-questions and concealed questions. Syntactically, a concealed question looks like a definite DP, but semantically, it works like a *wh*-question (see, e.g., Nathan 2006). In (20) and (21), the content of what Mary knows is expressed as a *wh*-question in (20) and as a concealed question in (21). (22) shows their parallel derivation.

(20) Mary know <u>how^u tall John$^\nu$ is</u>.
She thinks that Bill is shorter than that$_u$.

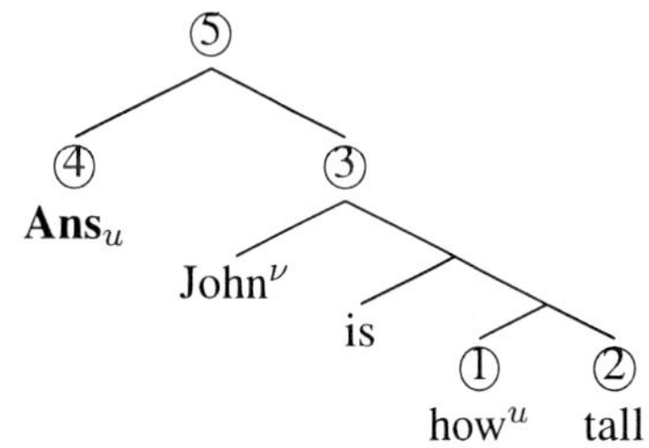

(21) Mary know <u>the^u height of John$^\nu$</u>.
She thinks that Bill is shorter than that$_u$.

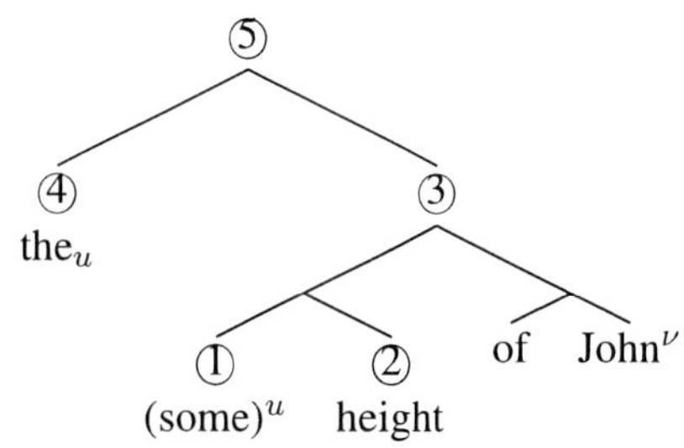

(22) ① $= \lambda g.\ \{g^{u\mapsto I} | \textsc{Interval}(I)\}$
② $= \lambda I \lambda x.\textsc{height}(x) \subseteq I$
(i.e., the height measurement of x falls into the interval I.)
③ $= \lambda g.\ \left\{g^{\substack{u\mapsto I \\ \nu\mapsto x}} | \textsc{height}(x) \subseteq I, x = \text{J}\right\}$
④ $= \mathbf{Ans}_u \overset{\text{def}}{=} \lambda m.\lambda g.$
$\{h \in m(g) \mid \neg\exists h' \in m(g)\,.\, h'(u) \subset h(u)\}$
⑤
$= \mathbf{Ans}_u(\lambda g.\ \left\{g^{\substack{u\mapsto I \\ \nu\mapsto x}} | \textsc{ht}(x) \subseteq I, x = \text{J}\right\})$
$= \lambda g.\ \left\{g^{\substack{u\mapsto I \\ \nu\mapsto x}} |\ I = \iota I[\textsc{ht}(\text{J}) \subseteq I], x = \text{J}\right\}$

In both cases, the semantic contribution of *the* and *how* can be considered two-fold. They (i) first introduce a dref in the domain of degrees or intervals (which supports cross-sentential anaphora later)[3] and (ii) then impose a definiteness test, lead-

[3] An interval is a convex set of degrees, e.g., $[5', 5']$, $[5', 6']$ (Schwarzchild and Wilkinson 2002; Zhang and Ling 2021).

ing to maximal informativeness.[4] Thus the most informative interval in which the height measurement of John falls is selected out (e.g., $[5'11'', 5'11'']$, if the measurement is very precise). In this case, since the domain of the dref is not a set of individuals, but a set of intervals, the specific implementation of $\mathbf{Ans}_u$ (see ④ in (22)) is not mereology-based.

3 Further extensions

Now I sketch out how the proposal can be extended to account for more question-related phenomena.

3.1 Strong vs. weak exhaustivity

Among various theories on question semantics, Partition Semantics (Groenendijk and Stokhof 1982, 1984, 1990) is motivated by a distinction between a strong vs. a weak exhaustive reading of sentences like (23).

Under the weak exhaustive reading, (23) means that Mary has the complete knowledge about all walkers (see (23a)). Under the strong exhaustive reading, (23) means that Mary has the complete knowledge about everyone in the domain, including all walkers and non-walkers (see (23b)).

(23) Mary knows <u>who^u walks</u>.

a. If x walks, Mary knows x walks. **W**

b. For each individual x in the domain, Mary knows whether x walks. **S**

To capture the strong exhaustive reading, Partition Semantics analyzes a question as a partition on possible worlds. The current proposal can also be extended to capture this strong exhaustive reading.

As shown in (24), the embedded *wh*-question in (23) is analyzed in the same way as a matrix *wh*-question, yielding the sum of all those who walk, which is assigned to u.

Then the part *Mary knows* works like a post-suppositional test, providing additional information on $g(u)$. This part is similar to a good short question (e.g., (1b)) in that their semantic contribution is based on and added to some definite item already established and restricted by the *wh*-question.

For the weak exhaustive reading, as shown in (25), $\mathbf{Mary\ knows}_{\text{weak}\ u}$ checks for each part of $g(u)$, x', whether the part-whole relation '$x' \sqsubseteq g(u)$' is known by Mary. For the strong exhaustive reading, as shown in (26), $\mathbf{Mary\ knows}_{\text{strong}\ u}$ checks (i) for each part of $g(u)$, x', whether the part-whole relation '$x' \sqsubseteq g(u)$' is known by Mary, and (ii) for each x' that is not part of $g(u)$, whether '$x' \not\sqsubseteq g(u)$' is known by Mary. In (25) and (26), $\mathfrak{Know}_{\mathfrak{M}}$ is of type $\langle tt \rangle$, a set of items of type t.

(24) $[\![(23)]\!] =$
$\mathbf{Mary\ knows}_u(\mathbf{Ans}_u([\![\text{who}^u \text{ walks}]\!]))$
$\mathbf{Ans}_u([\![\text{who}^u \text{ walks}]\!]) =$
$\lambda g.\ \{g^{u \mapsto x} | \ x = \Sigma x[\text{HMN}(x) \land \text{WALK}(x)]\}$

(25) **Weak exhaustivity reading**:
$\mathbf{Mary\ knows}_{\text{weak}\ u} \stackrel{\text{def}}{=} \lambda m.\lambda g.m(g)$ if $\forall x'[x' \sqsubseteq g(u) \rightarrow \mathfrak{Know}_{\mathfrak{M}}(x' \sqsubseteq g(u))]$
(i.e., for any x' in the domain, if x' walks, then Mary knows x' walks.)

(26) **Strong exhaustivity reading**:
$\mathbf{Mary\ knows}_{\text{strong}\ u} \stackrel{\text{def}}{=} \lambda m.\lambda g.m(g)$ if $\forall x'[x' \sqsubseteq g(u) \rightarrow \mathfrak{Know}_{\mathfrak{M}}(x' \sqsubseteq g(u))] \land \forall x'[x' \not\sqsubseteq g(u) \rightarrow \mathfrak{Know}_{\mathfrak{M}}(x' \not\sqsubseteq g(u))]$
(i.e., for any x' in the domain, Mary knows whether x' walks.)

Quantificational variability can be captured in the same way, as illustrated in (27) and (28). In (28), the test $\mathbf{Mary\ knows}_{\text{part}\ u}$ checks whether for some part of $g(u)$, x', the part-whole relation '$x' \sqsubseteq g(u)$' is known by Mary.

(27) **Quantificational variability**:
Mary partly knows <u>who^u walks</u>.

(28) $\mathbf{Mary\ knows}_{\text{part}\ u} \stackrel{\text{def}}{=} \lambda m.\lambda g.m(g)$ if $\exists x'[x' \sqsubseteq g(u) \land \mathfrak{Know}_{\mathfrak{M}}(x' \sqsubseteq g(u))]$

Under the current proposal, the question meaning itself and its analytical answer always remain the same (see (24)). What varies is what is included in Mary's knowledge. The current analysis also reflects the extensionality of knowledge: What is included in Mary's knowledge does not affect or change the answer to the *wh*-question itself.

Even if different possible worlds have different walkers, (i) the way how the analytical answer to a *wh*-question is characterized and (ii) the way how somebody's knowledge is connected to this analytical answer are stable across different possible worlds. Thus the meaning of sentences like (23) should be the same at every world, and the current analysis captures this stability.

3.2 Question coordination

Xiang (2021) points out that the traditional categorial approach to *wh*-questions is challenged by

[4] See Bumford (2017) for the idea that the meaning of *the* includes an indefinite part. This idea can be dated back to Russell (1905).

question coordination. For a sentence like (29), the traditional approach predicts that it has the same meaning as *Jenny knows who voted for Andy and Bill* (see (30)), and this prediction is inconsistent with our intuitive interpretation for (29).

(29) Jenny knows who^{u_1} voted for Andy and who^{u_2} voted for Bill. (see Xiang 2021)

(30) Traditional categorial approach:
$[\![$who voted for Andy and who voted for Bill$]\!]$
$= \lambda x.\text{VOTE}(x, \text{A}) \sqcap \lambda x.\text{VOTE}(x, \text{B})$
$= \lambda x.[\text{VOTE}(x, \text{A}) \wedge \text{VOTE}(x, \text{B})]$
$= [\![$who voted for Andy and Bill$]\!]$

Under the current analysis, for (29), the two *wh*-items each introduce a dref and different restrictions are applied to the two drefs respectively. Then two **Ans** operators are applied, selecting out the maximal drefs (see (31)). Finally, (32) shows that Jenny has the (weak) exhaustive knowledge about these two maximal drefs. In her knowledge, each dref is tracked separately.

(31) $\textbf{Ans}_{u_1}([\![\text{who}^{u_1} \text{ voted for Andy}]\!])$
$\wedge \textbf{Ans}_{u_2}([\![\text{who}^{u_2} \text{ voted for Bill}]\!])$
$= \lambda g.\{g^{\substack{u_1 \mapsto x \\ u_2 \mapsto y}} \mid x = \Sigma x[\text{HMN}(x) \wedge \text{VT}(x, \text{A})], y = \Sigma y[\text{HMN}(y) \wedge \text{VT}(y, \text{B})]\}$

(32) $\textbf{Jenny knows}_{\text{weak } u_1, u_2, \ldots} \stackrel{\text{def}}{=} \lambda m.\lambda g.m(g)$ if for each variable $u_i \in \{u_1, u_2, \ldots\}$, $\forall x'[x' \sqsubseteq g(u_i) \rightarrow \mathfrak{Know}_{\mathfrak{J}}(x' \sqsubseteq g(u_i))]$

3.3 *Wh*-conditionals

The above idea on question coordination can be further extended to sentences with multi *wh*-items.

(33) Who^{u} comes depends on who$^{\nu}$ is invited.

(34) $\textbf{depend-on}_{u,\nu} \stackrel{\text{def}}{=} \lambda m.\lambda g.m(g)$ if $\exists f.f(g(\nu)) = g(u)$

Sentence (33) addresses the correlation between the answers to two *wh*-questions. The answer to the question *who^{u} comes* correlates with or depends on the answer to the question *who$^{\nu}$ is invited.* As proposed in (34), $\textbf{depend-on}_{u,\nu}$ works as a post-suppositional test, checking whether there is a function f mapping the maximal dref assigned to ν, i.e., $g(v)$, to the maximal dref assigned to u, i.e., $g(u)$. Thus again $\textbf{depend-on}_{u,\nu}$ is like a short answer or *Mary knows* in that their semantic contribution is based on and added to existing definite items.

Wh-conditionals in Mandarin Chinese can be accounted for in exactly the same way.

According to Liu (2017); Xiang (2021); Li (2019, 2021), a *wh*-conditional sentence like (35) includes two questions, here *who^{u} loses* and *who$^{\nu}$ pays*, and the short answer to the first *wh*-question is equivalent to the short answer to the second one (cf. Xiang 2021). As shown in (36) and (37), this intuitive reading is naturally accounted for.

(35) Shéi^{u} shū-le, shéi$^{\nu}$ (jiù) qǐngkè
who lose-ASP who (then) pay
'For every person x, if x is the one losing the bet, x is the one paying.' (see Li 2021)

(36)
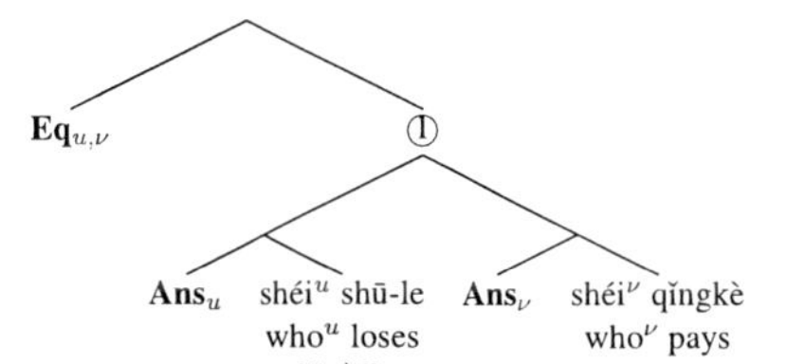

① $= \lambda g.\{g^{\substack{u \mapsto x \\ \nu \mapsto y}} \mid x = \Sigma x[\text{HMN}(x) \wedge \text{LOSE}(x)], y = \Sigma y[\text{HMN}(y) \wedge \text{PAY}(y)]\}$

(37) $\textbf{Eq}_{u,\nu} = \lambda m.\lambda g.m(g)$ if $g(u) = g(\nu)$

More general cases of *wh*-conditionals, including those involving degree questions, can also be accounted for. (38) means that the amount of food you eat determines the amount of money you pay, i.e., the answer to the first degree question determines the answer to the second one.

(38) chī duō-shǎo$^{u_1;\nu_1}$, fù duō-shǎo$^{u_2;\nu_2}$
eat how.much pay how.much
'How much (you) eat, how much (money you) pay.' (see Liu 2017; cf. Xiang 2021)

(39) $\lambda g.\{g^{\substack{u_1 \mapsto x, \nu_1 \mapsto I_1 \\ u_2 \mapsto y, \nu_2 \mapsto I_2}} \mid x = \Sigma x[\text{FD}(x)], y = \Sigma y[\text{MN}(y)], I_1 = \text{AM}(x), I_2 = \text{AM}(y)\}$

(40) $\textbf{determine}_{\nu_1,\nu_2} = \lambda m.\lambda g.m(g)$ if $\exists f.f(g(\nu_1)) = g(\nu_2)$

For (38), I assume that each degree question introduces two drefs: one in the domain of e (here x and y), and the other one in the domain of intervals (here I_1 and I_2). (39) shows that the most informative drefs are picked out: the mereologically maximal x and y, and the most informative amount measurement of x and y, i.e., I_1 and I_2. Obviously, I_1 and I_2 are the most informative answers to the two *wh*-questions in (38). Similar to (34), silent operator $\textbf{determine}_{\nu_1,\nu_2}$ works as a test, checking whether there is a context relevant function f that maps $g(\nu_1)$ to $g(\nu_2)$. The operator $\textbf{Eq}_{u,\nu}$ (37) can be considered a special case of the operator $\textbf{determine}_{\nu_1,\nu_2}$ in (40).

3.4 Question dependency

Syntactically, there are two subtypes of question dependency: **direct dependency** (see (41)) and **indirect dependency** (see (42)). Semantically, they have the same meaning. Based on their syntactic differences, Dayal (1994, 2016) advocate distinct analyses to derive their meaning. Here I follow this desideratum to address question dependency.

(41) Where^u does John think Mary is?

(42) What$^\nu$ does John think? Where^u is Mary?

As shown in (43), the derivation of direct dependency is straightforward. *Wh*-item *where*^{u} introduces a dref (which is a location), and the application of the definiteness test $\mathbf{Ans}_u$ is delayed until the matrix sentence level. Due to the selection requirement of *think*, roughly speaking, the embedded question should be something of type $\langle st \rangle$, and ⟦John thinks⟧ is of type $\langle st, t\rangle$, restricting items of type $\langle st \rangle$. Eventually, (41) denotes the most informative dref x such that John thinks Mary is in x. Obviously, this dref x does not necessarily satisfy the restriction '$\text{IN}(\text{Mary}, x, w)$' (in which w is a free variable). Thus the intensionality of attitude-reporting predicate *think* is captured.

(43)

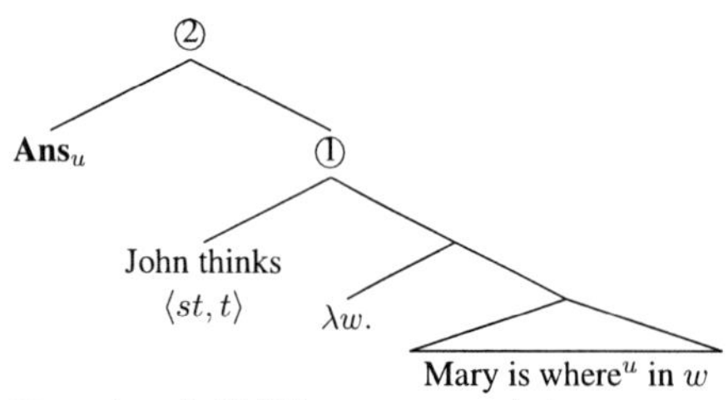

$① = \lambda g.\{g^{u\mapsto x} |\ \text{LOCATION}(x),$
$\text{JOHN-THINKS}(\lambda w.\text{IN}(\text{Mary}, x, w))\}$
$② = \lambda g.\{g^{u\mapsto x} |\ x = \iota x[\text{LCT}(x) \wedge$
$\text{JOHN-THINKS}(\lambda w.\text{IN}(\text{Mary}, x, w))]\}$

Then as shown in (44), for (42), I propose that *what*$^\nu$ introduces a dref of type $\langle st \rangle$, and *where*^{u} introduces a dref of type e. As shown in ⓑ, the part of the *what*$^\nu$ question denotes the most informative proposition p satisfying $\text{JOHN-THINKS}(p)$. Then as shown in ⓒ, the *where*^{u} question works as a test and provides further information on p, introducing a dref x and checking whether this most informative p entails a propositional that addresses Mary is somewhere. The rest is similar to the case of direct dependency. Eventually, (42) also denotes the most informative dref x such that John thinks Mary is in x, i.e., the same meaning as (41).

(44)

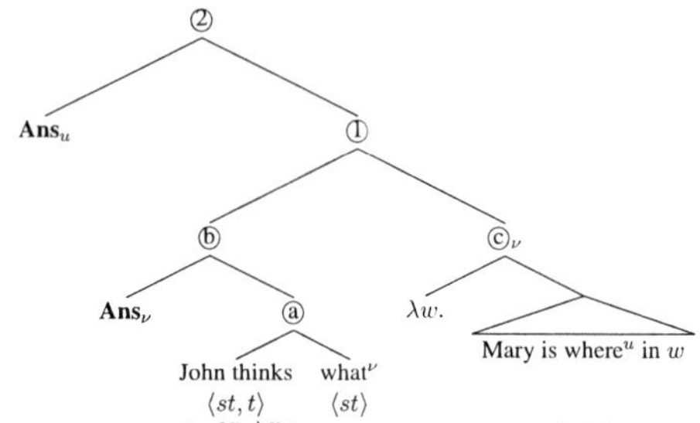

$ⓐ = \lambda g.\{g^{\nu\mapsto p} |\ \text{JOHN-THINKS}(p)\}$
$ⓑ = \mathbf{Ans}_\nu(ⓐ) =$
$\lambda g.\{g^{\nu\mapsto p} |\ p = \cap p[\text{JOHN-THINKS}(p)]\}$
$ⓒ_\nu = [\![\lambda w.\textbf{Mary is where}^u \textbf{ in } w]\!]_\nu =$
$\lambda m.\lambda g.m(g)$ if $g(u) \mapsto x$ s.t. $\text{LCT}(x) \wedge$
$g(\nu) \subseteq \lambda w.\text{IN}(\text{Mary}, x, w)$
$① = \lambda g.\{g^{\substack{u\mapsto x\\ \nu\mapsto p}} |\ \text{LC}(x), p = \cap p[\text{J-T}(p)],$
$\text{JOHN-THINKS}(\lambda w.\text{IN}(\text{Mary}, x, w))\}$
$② = \lambda g.\{g^{\substack{u\mapsto x\\ \nu\mapsto p}} |\ p = \cap p[\text{J-T}(p)], x =$
$\Sigma x[\text{LCT}(x) \wedge \text{J-T}(\lambda w.\text{IN}(\text{Mary}, x, w))]\}$

The current analysis of question dependency is still in line with Karttunen (1977): A *wh*-question denotes its complete true answer, not its possible answers (see Section 2.3). With this dynamics semantics implementation, the derivation always starts with non-determinate alternatives, and it is the application of **Ans** operators that results in relativized definite items that constitute complete true answers. In (44), $\mathbf{Ans}_u$ is not applied on ⓒ, but delayed until discourse level. thus the derivation never yields a Hamblin set for *where*^{u} *is Mary*.

3.5 Multi-*wh*-questions

A multi-*wh*-question has two readings, e.g.,

(45) Which girl read which book?

a. **Single-pair reading**:
Anna read *Anna Karenina*.

b. **Pair-list reading**: Anna read *Anna Karenina*; Emma read *Madame Bovary*; Jane read *Jane Eyre*.

The single-pair reading (45a) is easy to derive. In (46), atomic drefs x and y are introduced, and the operator $\mathbf{Ans}_{u,\nu}$ checks whether they are unique.

(46)

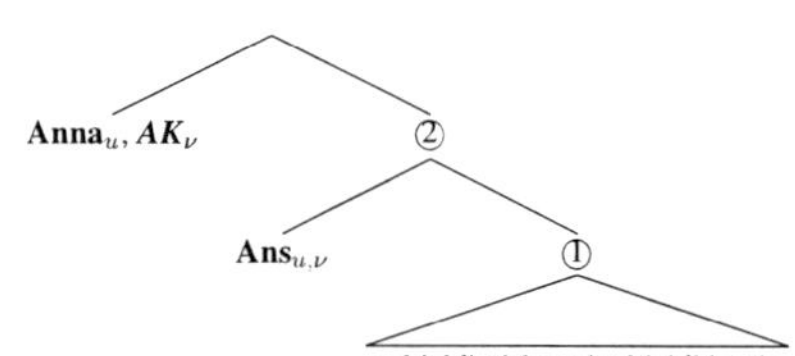

$① = \lambda g.\left\{g^{\substack{u\mapsto x\\ \nu\mapsto y}} |\text{GL}(x), \text{BK}(y), \text{RD}(x, y)\right\}$

(drefs x and y are atomic here.)
Single-pair reading: $\textbf{Ans}_{u,\nu} = \lambda m.\lambda g.m(g)$ if $|\{g(u) \mid g \in m(g)\}| = 1$ and $|\{g(\nu) \mid g \in m(g)\}| = 1$.
(i.e., there is a unique girl-reader and a unique book read by a girl.)
$② = \lambda g.\{g^{\substack{u \mapsto x \\ \nu \mapsto y}} | x = \iota x[\text{GL}(x) \wedge \text{RD}(x, y)], y = \iota y[\text{BK}(y) \wedge \text{RD}(x, y)]\}$
($\textbf{Anna}_u$, $\textbf{\textit{AK}}_\nu$ bring more tests on drefs.)

For the pair-list reading (45b), its short answer can be considered a function written as a set of ordered pairs: i.e., $f = \{\langle \text{A}, \textit{AK}\rangle, \langle \text{E}, \textit{MB}\rangle, \langle \text{J}, \textit{JE}\rangle\}$ (see Schlenker 2006; Brasoveanu 2011; Bumford 2015). Another observation is that pair-list reading is different from single-pair reading in supporting cross-sentential anaphora (see (47) vs. (48)).

(47) Which^u girl read which$^\nu$ book? Does she$_u$ like it$_\nu$? ✓ single-pair; # pair-list

(48) Which^u girl read which$^\nu$ book? Do they$_u$ like their$_u$ book / # it$_\nu$? ✓ pair-list

Thus the pair-list reading of (45) amounts to 'what is the function f s.t. for each girl x' who read, $f(x')$ is all the books x' read and $|f(x')| = 1$'. In (49), *which^u girl* introduces a (potentially plural) dref x, and *which$^\nu$* (*book*) introduces a functional dref f, mapping each atomic x' to the book-sum x' read. I assume that a hidden distributivity operator DIST is responsible for the singularity of *girl*. $\textbf{Ans}_u$ selects out the maximal sum of girl-readers. $\textbf{Ans}_\nu$ checks the singularity of *book*, i.e., whether for each x', $|f(x')| = 1$. If so, f is the short answer.[5]

(49)
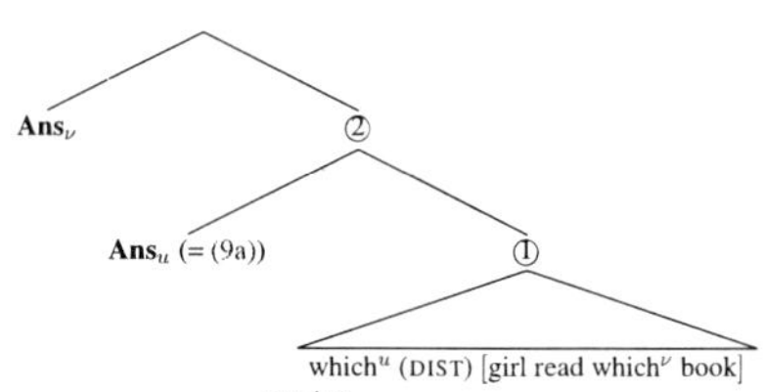

$① = \lambda g.\{g^{\substack{u \mapsto x \\ \nu \mapsto f}} | \text{G}(x), \forall x'_{\text{ATM}} \sqsubseteq x[f(x') = \Sigma f(x')[\text{BK}(f(x')) \wedge \text{RD}(x', f(x'))]\}$
$\textbf{Ans}_\nu = \lambda m.\lambda g.m(g)$ if $\forall x'[x'_{\text{ATM}} \sqsubseteq g(u) \rightarrow |g(\nu)(x')| = 1]$

4 Comparison with recent works

Among recent works, there are heated discussions on how to represent the drefs introduced by *wh*-items, how to have access to short answers, etc. These issues motivate new approaches to questions, incorporating insights from dynamic semantics or categorial approaches (e.g., Krifka 2001; Xiang 2021; Li 2019, 2021; Dotlačil and Roelofsen 2019, 2021). The current work joins this trend of research and has a similar empirical coverage.[6]

Compared to other recent works, the current work is distinguished in at least two aspects. First, conceptually, it provides a new perspective on answerhood, teasing apart the analytically invariant, definite part and the part that contributes new information. New information is considered tests at another layer, providing further description for the analytically invariant part. Thus even though a *wh*-question might be answered with different informative short answers in different possible worlds, the analytical definite dref remains stable. Consequently, in analyzing question phenomena, we can just start with this complete true answer, and various phenomena address what/how additional information is related to this analytical answer.

Second, empirically, the current approach brings a more unified treatment for *wh*-questions raised on different domains (e.g., entities, scalar values like degrees or intervals). Specific implementation of definiteness tests is based on the same idea of maximizing informativeness. We never need to loop over possible answers in the domain of *wh*-items, which is difficult for domains of non-entities.

5 Summary

This paper explores a post-suppositional view on *wh*-questions and answers. I analyze *wh*-items along with items like modified numerals: their semantic contribution all involves dref introduction and definiteness tests. Based on this, for answers to *wh*-questions, we can separate the invariant, analytical part, and the new information part. The new information part further serves as tests on the invariant part. This papers also sketches out how a series of related phenomena are analyzed. Further development and refinement is left for future work.

References

Adrian Brasoveanu. 2011. Sentence-internal different as quantifier-internal anaphora. *Linguistics and philosophy*, pages 93–168.

[5]For a question like *which girl smiled*, based on how it supports cross-sentential anaphora (see (47) vs. (48)), I assume that only an analysis like (46), but not like (49), is possible.

[6]In addition to the phenomena discussed in this paper, the current perspective on *wh*-questions also provides an account for focus intervention effects (see Zhang 2023b).

Adrian Brasoveanu. 2013. Modified numerals as post-suppositions. *Journal of Semantics*, 30(2):155–209.

Dylan Bumford. 2015. Incremental quantification and the dynamics of pair-list phenomena. *Semantics and Pragmatics*, 8 (9):1–70.

Dylan Bumford. 2017. Split-scope definites: Relative superlatives and Haddock descriptions. *Linguistics and Philosophy*, 40(6):549–593.

Ivano Caponigro. 2003. *Free not to ask: On the semantics of free relatives and wh-words cross-linguistically*. Ph.D. thesis, UCLA.

Ivano Caponigro. 2004. The semantic contribution of *wh*-words and type shifts: Evidence from free relatives crosslinguistically. In *Semantics and linguistic theory*, volume 14, pages 38–55.

Simon Charlow. 2014. *On the semantics of exceptional scope*. Ph.D. thesis, NYU.

Simon Charlow. 2017. Post-suppositions and semantic theory. *Journal of semantics* (in press).

Gennaro Chierchia and Ivano Caponigro. 2013. Questions on questions and free relatives. In *Sinn und Bedeutung*, volume 18.

Ileana Comorovski. 2013. *Interrogative phrases and the syntax-semantics interface*, volume 59. Springer Science & Business Media.

Veneeta Dayal. 1996. *Locality in WH quantification: Questions and relative clauses in Hindi*. Springer Science & Business Media.

Veneeta Dayal. 2016. *Questions*, volume 4. Oxford University Press.

Veneeta Srivastav Dayal. 1994. Scope marking as indirect *wh*-dependency. *Natural language semantics*, 2(2):137–170.

Jakub Dotlačil and Floris Roelofsen. 2019. Dynamic inquisitive semantics: Anaphora and questions. In *Proceedings of sinn und bedeutung*, volume 23 (1), pages 365–382.

Jakub Dotlačil and Floris Roelofsen. 2021. A dynamic semantics of single-*wh* and multiple-*wh* questions. In *Semantics and Linguistic Theory*, volume 30, pages 376–395.

Jeroen Groenendijk and Martin Stokhof. 1982. Semantic analysis of *wh*-complements. *Linguistics and philosophy*, pages 175–233.

Jeroen Groenendijk and Martin Stokhof. 1984. On the semantics of questions and the pragmatics of answers. In *Varieties of Formal Semantics: Proceedings of the Fourth Amsterdam Colloquium*, pages 143–170.

Jeroen Groenendijk and Martin Stokhof. 1990. Partitioning logical space. Annotated handout for *ESSLLI* 2, Leuven.

Charles L Hamblin. 1973. Questions in montague grammar. *Foundations of Language*, 10:41–53.

Roland Hausser and Dietmar Zaefferer. 1978. Questions and answers in a context-dependent montague grammar. In *Formal semantics and pragmatics for natural languages*, pages 339–358. Springer.

Pauline Jacobson. 2016. The short answer: Implications for direct compositionality (and vice versa). *Language*, 92 (2):331–375.

Lauri Karttunen. 1977. Syntax and semantics of questions. *Linguistics and philosophy*, 1:3–44.

Manfred Krifka. 2001. For a structured meaning account of questions and answers. In *Audiatur Vox Sapientia. A Festschrift for Arnim von Stechow*, volume 52, pages 287–319.

Haoze Li. 2019. Deriving short answers from hamblin sets: A case study of mandarin wh-conditionals. In *Semantics and linguistic theory*, volume 29, pages 138–159.

Haoze Li. 2021. Mandarin wh-conditionals: A dynamic question approach. *Natural Language Semantics*, 29(3):401–451.

Mingming Liu. 2017. *Varieties of alternatives: Focus particles and wh-expressions in Mandarin*. Berlin and Beijing: Springer and Peking University.

Lance Edward Nathan. 2006. *On the interpretation of concealed questions*. Ph.D. thesis, MIT.

Bertrand Russell. 1905. On denoting. *Mind*, 14(56):479–493.

Philippe Schlenker. 2006. Scopal independence: A note on branching and wide scope readings of indefinites and disjunctions. *Journal of Semantics*, 23(3):281–314.

Roger Schwarzchild and Karina Wilkinson. 2002. Quantifiers in comparatives: A semantics of degree based on intervals. *Natural language semantics*, 10:1–41.

Yimei Xiang. 2021. A hybrid categorial approach to question composition. *Linguistics and Philosophy*, 44(3):587–647.

Linmin Zhang. 2023a. Cumulative reading, QUD, and maximal informativeness. To appear in the *Proceedings of LENLS 19*.

Linmin Zhang. 2023b. Focus intervention effects revisited: A semantics-pragmatics approach. To appear in the *Japanese/Korean Linguistics 30*.

Linmin Zhang and Jia Ling. 2021. The semantics of comparatives: A difference-based approach. *Journal of Semantics*, 38(2):249–303.

Referential Transparency and Inquisitivity

Jonathan Ginzburg
Université Paris Cité, CNRS
Laboratoire de Linguistique Formelle
yonatan.ginzburg@u-paris.fr

Andy Lücking
Université Paris Cité, CNRS
Laboratoire de Linguistique Formelle
and
Goethe University Frankfurt
lueckin g@em.uni-frankfurt.de

Abstract

The paper extends a *referentially transparent* approach which has been successfully applied to the analysis of declarative quantified NPs to *wh*-phrases. This uses data from dialogical phenomena such as clarification interaction, anaphora, and incrementality as a guide to the design of *wh*-phrase meanings.

1 Introduction

An alternative to Generalized Quantifier Theory (GQT) has recently been developed in terms of *Referential Transparency Theory* (RTT; Lücking and Ginzburg, 2022). RTT draws its main motivation from data of natural language use as observed in dialogical interactions, where higher-order denotations postulated by GQT do not seem to be confirmed. Hence, RTT pursues a witness-based approach to quantification, which arguably simplifies the representation of quantification phenomena.

In this paper, we extend this to questions. This is *prima facie* tricky because in contrast to QNPs *Wh*-phrases (WhPs) are never referential.[1] Indeed a crucial difference between declarative and interrogative quantified meaning is that the former involves *predication*—giving rise to descriptive potential, whereas the latter involves *abstraction*—giving rise to predicational potential. Phenomena we discuss includes the following:

Clarificational potential: Data from clarification allows for a considerable strengthening of compositionality, the classical syntax-semantics interface desideratum. This via the Reprise Content Hypothesis (RCH) due to (Purver and Ginzburg, 2004) They distinguish different kinds of reprise fragments, including *intended meaning* requests, that is, reprise fragments that follow the template "A: $\ldots u_1 \ldots$ B: u_1?" exemplified in (2). Purver and Ginzburg (2004) show further that reprise fragments of the *intended meaning* type, at least when they address a non-sentential constituent, do not query pragmatically inferred material but are restricted to direct semantic content. On the basis of this they posit the *Reprise Content Hypothesis* whose strong version is given in (1):

(1) **Reprise Content Hypothesis:** A reprise fragment question queries exactly the standard semantic content of the fragment being reprised.

Whereas non-interrogative QNPs allow for clarification questions relating to their witnesses (but not to properties of properties, as would be expected in GQ accounts), *wh*-phrases allow only for clarification of their restriction property (not to any propositional entities, as might be expected by GQ accounts of interrogatives common in Type–driven Categorial Grammar (Vermaat, 2006; Mihaliček and Pollard, 2012)).[2]

(2) a. A: Most students came to the party. B: Most students? A: Yes, all but Tristan and Isolde.

[1] Of course there are languages where the same form, albeit with distinct intonation, plays a double or even triple role such as Hebrew 'eyze' which serves as a quantificational, interrogative and exclamative determiner:

(i) eyze yeladim azvu(./?/!)
Some/Which/what child-pl left
Some children left./Which children left?/What children left!

Our account will enable us to capture the core similarities between these uses, but crucially also the differences, as we demonstrate in an extended version of this paper.

[2] See (Purver, 2004) for corpus examples of clarification exchanges concerning *wh*-phrases, though he does not discuss examples like our (constructed) (2c,d).

Proceedings of the 4th Workshop on Inquisitiveness Below and Beyond the Sentence Boundary (InqBnB4), pages 11–20
June 20, 2023. ©2023 Association for Computational Linguistics

b. A: Everyone supports the proposals. B: Everyone? A: All the ministers.

c. A: Who should we contact for help? B: Who? A: A lawyer or a psychologist?/#Everyone except Tristan and Isolde.

d. A: When are you leaving? B: When? A: What day./#Saturday.

A similar point can be made for intensional argument roles of verbs, which allow for clarification without expectation of witnesses (Cooper, 2013b):

(3) A: Sam is looking for the trainset.
B: What trainset?
A: The one he was promised for Christmas (Cooper, 2013b),

Anaphoric potential: *wh*-phrases allow for discourse anaphora, though without a referential commitment:

(4) a. A: Who will support the proposal? Will they reveal themselves before the vote? B: No one. A: Yeah that makes sense.

b. A: Where are you going? Can we contact you there?

The same holds for intensional argument roles of verbs:

(5) a. Charlie wants a train for her birthday. Ideally it should be light blue.

Incremental potential: input is processed word by word (and indeed at a higher, sub-lexical latency). Utterances with QNPs are understood incrementally (Urbach et al., 2015), as exemplified also in (6a,b). Although we are not aware of similar empirical studies for *wh*-phrases, (6c,d) suggests that this is the case as well:[3]

(6) a. A: Everyone ... B: Who?

b. A: [enters class] No students ... Oh, they're hiding.

c. A: Who... B: What are you going to ask me now?

d. A: Which student... B: In what class?

[3]For an interesting discussion of incremental interpretation of *wh*-questions, though not in a dialogical setting see (Hopmans, 2019).

Approaches which treat *wh*-phrases as mediated via an operation like Quantifier Raising, where a quantifier is moved out of its syntactic surface position into another position in logical form or more generally involve long-distance binding (Xiang, 2021), seems to be a serious obstacle to this empirical fact.

Answerhood: the substantive semantic contribution of *wh*-phrases is the answerhood conditions they give rise to, the details of which are discussed in section 2.

Response space: any dialogical theory of meaning needs to account for the class of responses a given utterance type gives rise to. In the case of questions there exists detailed empirical and formal work we build on (Ginzburg et al., 2022), briefly summarized in section 2.

An example that combines these aspects of *wh*-phrase meaning is in figure 1, where the exophoric context triggers the bare *wh*–clarification question, which give rise to the short answer.

Figure 1: (Context: Harden gets called for a foul) Harden: *Who, me?*

In section 2, we sketch a theory of questions, answerhood, and responses. In section 3, we develop our account of *wh*-phrase meaning, which is applied to the initial data in section 4.

2 A KoS-TTR theory of questions

Our explication is formulated using the frameworks of Type Theory with Records (TTR; Cooper and Ginzburg, 2015; Cooper, 2023) (for the semantic ontology) and KoS (Ginzburg, 2012; Ginzburg et al., 2022) (for the theory of dialogue context).

2.1 Basic semantic notions

We will assume a view of questions as propositional functions, a view apparently initiated by Ajdukiewicz (1926), developed significantly in Kubinski (1960), and subsequently shared and further developed by a number of different approaches, e.g., Krifka (2001).

We adopt an implementation of this view within the framework of TTR. The starting point, hence, is the notion of a proposition in TTR. Propositions are construed as typing relations between records (situations) and record types (situation types), or Austinian propositions (Austin, 1961; Barwise and Etchemendy, 1987); more formally:

(7) a. Propositions are records of type

$$\text{Prop} = \begin{bmatrix} \text{sit} & : \textit{Rec} \\ \text{sit-type} & : \textit{RecType} \end{bmatrix}.$$

b. $\text{p} = \begin{bmatrix} \text{sit} & = s \\ \text{sit-type} & = T \end{bmatrix}$ is true iff *p.sit* : *p.sit-type*

i.e., $s : T$ —the situation s is of the type T.

Similarly, we will model questions as records comprising two fields, a situation and a function (Ginzburg et al., 2014). The role of *wh*-words on this view is to specify the domains of these functions; in the case of polar questions there is no restriction, hence the function component of such a question is a constant function. (8) exemplifies this for a unary 'who' question and a polar question:

(8) a. $\textit{Who} = \begin{bmatrix} x_1 : \textit{Ind} \\ \text{c1} : \text{person}(x_1) \end{bmatrix};$

b. *Whether* = *Rec*;

c. 'Who runs?' $\mapsto$

$$\begin{bmatrix} \text{sit} = r_1 \\ \text{abstr} = f{:}\textit{Who}(\begin{bmatrix} \text{c} : \text{run}(r_1.x_1) \end{bmatrix}) \end{bmatrix};$$

d. 'Whether Bo runs?' $\mapsto$

$$\begin{bmatrix} \text{sit} = r_1 \\ \text{abstr} = f{:}\textit{Whether}(\begin{bmatrix} \text{c} : \text{run(b)} \end{bmatrix}) \end{bmatrix}$$

Austinian questions can be conjoined and disjoined though not negated. We view this as an advantage over inquisitive approaches which overgenerate in allowing interrogatives to be negated. The definition for con-/disjunction is as follows:

(9)
$$\begin{bmatrix} \text{sit} & = & s \\ \text{abstr} & = & f : T_1\ (T_2) \end{bmatrix} \quad \wedge \quad (\vee) \quad \begin{bmatrix} \text{sit} & = & s \\ \text{abstr} & = & f : T_3\ (T_4) \end{bmatrix} =$$
$$\begin{bmatrix} \text{sit} = \text{s} \\ \text{abstr} = f{:}\begin{bmatrix} \text{left}{:}T_1 \\ \text{right}{:}T_3 \end{bmatrix} \\ (q_1(s.\text{left}) \wedge (\vee) q_2(s.\text{right})) \end{bmatrix}$$

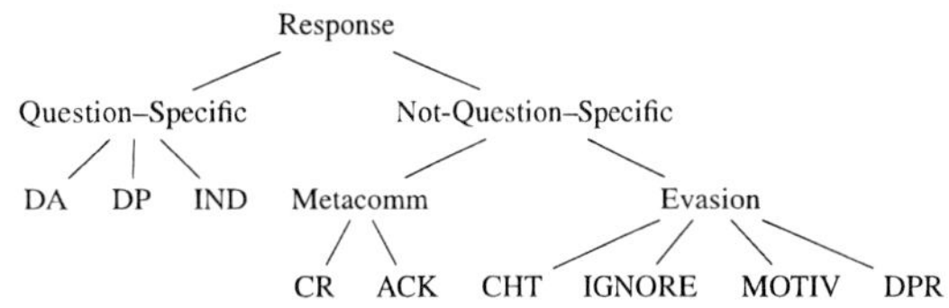

Figure 2: Proposed response space of questions

2.2 Response Space

We assume the following theory of the response space of queries, due to Ginzburg et al. (2022). This amounts to the following general types of responses (see Figure 2):

1. Question–Specific: DirectAnswers (DA), InDirectAnswers (IND) and Dependent Questions (DP):
   (a) Answerhood
   (b) Dependent questions (A: Who should we invite? B: Who is in town?)
2. Metacommunicative Responses:
   (a) Clarification Responses (CR)
   (b) Acknowledgements (ACK)
3. Evasion responses:
   (a) Ignore (address the situation, but not the question)
   (b) Change the topic (CHT; 'Answer *my* question')
   (c) Motive ('Why do you ask?')
   (d) Difficult to provide a response (DPR).

The basic notion of context we adopt is via each participant's view of publicized context, the *dialogue gameboard* (DGB), whose basic make up is given in (10):

(10)
$$\begin{bmatrix} \text{spkr} & : \textit{Ind} \\ \text{addr} & : \textit{Ind} \\ \text{utt-time} & : \textit{Time} \\ \text{c-utt} & : \text{addressing(spkr,addr,utt-time)} \\ \text{facts} & : \textit{set(Prop)} \\ \text{vis-sit} & = \begin{bmatrix} \text{foa} : \textit{Ind} \vee \textit{Rec} \end{bmatrix} : \textit{RecType} \\ \text{pending} & : \textit{list(LocProp)} \\ \text{moves} & : \textit{list(IllocProp)} \\ \text{qud} & : \textit{poset(Question)} \end{bmatrix}$$

Here *facts* represents the shared assumptions of the interlocutors—identified with a set of propositions.

Dialogue moves that are in the process of being grounded or under clarification are the elements of the *pending* list; already grounded moves are moved to the *moves* list. Within *moves* the first element has a special status given its use to capture adjacency pair coherence and it is referred to as *LatestMove*. The current question under discussion is tracked in the QUD field, whose data type is a partially ordered set (*poset*). *Vis-sit* represents the visual situation of an agent, including his or her visual focus of attention (*foa*), which can be an object (*Ind*), or a situation or event. We call a mapping between DGB types a *conversational rule*—Conversational rules are the means for specifying how DGBs evolve. The types specifying its domain and its range we dub, respectively, the *pre(conditions)* and the *effects*, both of which are subtypes of DGBType: they apply to a subclass of records that constitute possible DGBs and modify them to records that constitute possible DGBs. Conversational rules are written here in a form where the preconditions represent information specific to the preconditions of this particular interaction type and the effects represent those aspects of the preconditions that have changed.

The first conversational rule we formulate relates to the basic effect a query has on the DGB—as a consequence of a query a question becomes the maximal element of QUD:

(11) Ask QUD-incrementation: given a question q and Ask(A, B, q) being the LatestMove, one can update QUD with q as MaxQUD.

$$\begin{bmatrix} \text{pre} & : & \begin{bmatrix} \text{q} & : \textit{Question} \\ \text{LatestMove} = \text{Ask(spkr, addr, q)} & : \textit{LocProp} \end{bmatrix} \\ \text{effects} & : & \begin{bmatrix} \text{QUD} = \left\langle \text{q, pre.QUD} \right\rangle : & \textit{poset(Question)} \end{bmatrix} \end{bmatrix}$$

Before we consider how question–specific responses get accommodated, we turn to a discussion of answerhood.

2.3 Answerhood

Descriptively the *simple* answers to questions are the range of the propositional abstract, plus their negations.

(12) a. SimpleAns(p?) = $\{p, \neg p\}$;

b. SimpleAns($\lambda x.P(x)$) = $\{P(a), P(b), \ldots, \neg P(a), \neg P(b) \ldots\}$

More formally, an *atomic answer* p is a proposition for which there is a record r such that p is a proposition whose *sit* is identical to the question's *sit* and such that applying the question's *abstr* to r yields p's *sit-type*:

(13) AtomAns =

$$\begin{bmatrix} \text{p} & : \textit{Prop} \\ \text{q} & : \textit{Question} \\ \text{p.sit = q.sit} & : \textit{Rec} \\ \text{p.sit-type = q.abstr(p.sit)} & : \textit{RecType} \end{bmatrix}$$

A *negative* atomic answer p is a proposition for which there is a record r such that p is a proposition whose *sit* is identical to the question's *sit* and such that negating the application of the question's *abstr* to r yields p's *sit-type*:

(14) NegAtomAns =

$$\begin{bmatrix} \text{p} & : \textit{Prop} \\ \text{q} & : \textit{Question} \\ \text{p.sit = q.sit} & : \textit{Rec} \\ \text{p.sit-type} = \neg\text{q.abstr(p.sit)} & : \textit{RecType} \end{bmatrix}$$

To exemplify:

(15) a. Take r_1 : *Who* (cf. (8a)), e.g., r_1 = $\begin{bmatrix} \text{x}_1 = \text{a} \\ \text{c1 = PersObs1} \\ \ldots \end{bmatrix}$, then p_1= $\begin{bmatrix} \text{sit} = r_1 \\ \text{sit-type} = \text{abstr}(r_1) = \begin{bmatrix} \text{c} : \neg\ \text{run(a)} \end{bmatrix} \end{bmatrix}$ ('a does not run') is a negative *atomic* answer to the question 'who runs'.

b. Take any record r_1, then p_1 = $\begin{bmatrix} \text{sit} = r_1 \\ \text{sit-type} = \text{abstr}(r_1) = \begin{bmatrix} \text{c} : \neg\text{run(b)} \end{bmatrix} \end{bmatrix}$ is the only negative *atomic* answer to the question 'whether B runs'.

The type of negative answers, however, will be slightly revised in adopting answerhood to RTT in section 3.

A *simple* answer is an answer that is either atomic or negative atomic: p is a simple answer to q if r_0 : *AtomAns* and p = $r_0.p$ and q = $r_0.q$ or r_0 : *NegAtomAns* and p = $r_0.p$ and q = $r_0.q$:

(16) SimpleAns =

$$\begin{bmatrix} r_0 : \textit{AtomAns} \vee \textit{NegAtomAns} \\ \text{p} = r_0\text{.p} : \textit{Prop} \\ \text{q} = r_0\text{.q} : \textit{Question} \end{bmatrix}$$

In fact, *simple answerhood*, though it has good coverage in practice, is not sufficient. It does not accommodate conditional, weakly modalized, and quantificational answers, all of which are pervasive in actual linguistic use (Ginzburg and Sag, 2000).

Thus, we suggest that the semantic notion relevant to direct answerhood is the relation *aboutness*—a relation between propositions and questions that any speaker of a given language can recognize, independently of domain knowledge and of the goals underlying an interaction.

The most detailed discussion of Aboutness we are aware of is (Ginzburg and Sag, 2000, pp. 129–149), which offers (17a) (reformulated here in TTR as Austinian questions). This requires the situational type component of the proposition to be a subtype of the join of the situational type of the question's simple answer set. As it stands, this definition allows in principle very informationally strong types as direct answers, since nothing bounds the proposition from above. Plausible upper bounds for direct answerhood familiar in the semantics of questions from the classic proposal of (Karttunen, 1977) are the meets of the question's atomic and negative atomic answer set.[4] This condition is formulated in (17b):

(17) For $p = \begin{bmatrix} \text{sit} = \text{s}_1 \\ \text{sit-type} = \text{T}_1 \end{bmatrix} : \textit{Prop},$

$q = \begin{bmatrix} \text{sit} = \text{s}_1 \\ \text{abstr} = \text{r} : \text{T}_2(\text{T}_3) \end{bmatrix} : \textit{Question}$

a. $\textit{About}(p, q)$ holds iff $T_1 \sqsubseteq \bigvee\{T \mid \exists p'[p' : \textit{Prop} \wedge \textit{SimpleAns}(p', q) \wedge T = p'.\text{sit-type}]\}$

b. $\textit{DirectAns}(p, q)$ holds iff $\textit{About}(p, q)$ and either

(i) $\bigwedge \textit{AtomAns}(q) \sqsubseteq T_1$

or

(ii) $\bigwedge \textit{NegAtomAns}(q) \sqsubseteq T_1$

For reasons of space, we omit discussion here of indirect answers and dependent questions, which figure in the following conversational rule, which is the main engine in driving question–specific responses:

(18) a. Given $r : \textit{Question} \vee \textit{Prop}$, $q : \textit{Question}$, $\textit{dgb} : \textit{DGBType}$, QSpecific$(r, q, \textit{dgb})$ iff $\textit{DirectAns}(r, q) \vee \textit{IndirectAns}(r, q, \textit{dgb}) \vee \textit{Depend}(q, r)$

[4]For a polar question $p?$ the meets of the question's atomic and negative atomic answer set are respectively p and $\neg p$, whereas for a *wh*–question $\lambda x.P(x)$ (e.g., 'who left') they are respectively $\bigwedge P(a_i)$ ('Bo left and Millie left ...'), whereas $\bigwedge \neg P(a_i)$ ('Bo did not leave and Millie did not leave ..., i.e., equivalent to 'No one left').

b. QSPEC =

$$\begin{bmatrix} \text{pre} : \begin{bmatrix} \text{QUD} = \langle \text{q}, \text{Q} \rangle : \textit{poset(Question)} \end{bmatrix} \\ \text{effects} : \begin{bmatrix} \text{spkr} = \text{pre.spkr} \vee \text{pre.addr} : \textit{Ind} \\ \text{addr} : \textit{Ind} \\ \text{c}_{\text{addr}} : \neq(\text{addr,spkr}) \\ \text{p} : \textit{Prop} \vee \textit{Question} \\ \text{c1} : \text{QSpecific(p,q,pre)} \end{bmatrix} \end{bmatrix}$$

Ginzburg and Cooper (2004); Purver (2004); Ginzburg (2012) show how to account for the main classes of clarification requests using rule schemas of the form "if u is the interrogative utterance and u_0 is a constituent of u, allow responses that are *co-propositional*[5] with the clarification question $\text{CQ}^i(u0)$ into QUD.", where '$\text{CQ}^i(u0)$' is one of the three types of clarification question (repetition, confirmation, intended content) specified with respect to $u0$.

For instance, responses such as (2) can be explicated in terms of the schema in (19):

(19) if A's utterance u is yet to be grounded and u_0 is a sub-utterance of u, QUD can be updated with the question *What did A mean by* u_0*?*

More formally: the issue q_0, *What did A mean by* u_0*?*, for a constituent u_0 of the maximally pending utterance, A its speaker, can become the maximal element of QUD, licensing follow up utterances that are CoPropositional with q_0.[6]

(20) Parameter identification:

$$\begin{bmatrix} \text{pre} : \begin{bmatrix} \text{MaxPENDING} = \begin{bmatrix} \text{sit} = u \\ \text{sit-type} = T_u \end{bmatrix} : \textit{LocProp} \\ \text{A} = \text{u.dgb-params.spkr} : \textit{Ind} \\ u_0 : \textit{Sign} \\ \text{c1} : \text{member}(u_0\text{,u.constits}) \end{bmatrix} \\ \text{effects} : \begin{bmatrix} \text{MaxQUD} = \lambda x.\text{Mean}(\text{A},u_0,\text{x}) : \textit{Question} \\ \text{LatestMove} : \textit{LocProp} \\ \text{c1} : \text{CoPropositional(LatestMove.cont, MaxQUD)} \end{bmatrix} \end{bmatrix}$$

(21) a. $\lambda x.\textit{Mean}(A, u_0, x)$

[5]Here *CoPropositionality* for two questions means that, modulo their domain, the questions involve similar answers: for instance 'Whether Bo left?', 'Who left?', and 'Which student left?' (assuming Bo is a student) are all co-propositional. More precisely, two questions q_1 and q_2 are copropositional iff there exist a record r such that $q_1(r) = q_2(r)$.

[6]Assuming a propositional function view of questions, CoPropositionality allows in propositions from the range of $\textit{Range}(q_0)$ and questions whose range intersects $\textit{Range}(q_0)$. Since CoPropositionality is reflexive, this means in particular that the inferred clarification question is a possible follow up utterance, as are confirmations and corrections, as exemplified in (21).

b. ?Mean(A,u_0,b) ('Did you mean Bo')

c. Mean(A,u_0,c) ('You meant Chris')

The formulation of this rule is based on the existence of a feature CONSTITS which tracks all the constituents of an utterance and therefore licences clarification of all constituents down to the word level. It presupposes the existence of a relation $Mean$ that holds between the speaker of an utterance, the utterance, and the intended content. In general, this has been identified with the value instantiated by dgb-params (on a distinguished label 'x') for that utterance:

(22) Mean(A,u,c) iff u.dgb-param.spkr = A and u.dgb-param.x = c

This definition was motivated by the assumption that what gets queried in intended content CRs is the intended instantiation of contextual parameters.

3 An RTT theory of WhP meaning

As we have suggested, building on much past work, QNPs have more duties than merely contributing to truth conditions: QNPs act as antecedents for anaphoric expressions, they supply verbal affiliates of co-speech gestures, and they are objects of discourse dynamics which becomes apparent in terms of acceptance or clarification requests (we restrict attention here to nominals, but the conditions generalize cross-categorially):

(23) **Referential Transparency**: a semantic representation for an NP is *referentially transparent* if

a. it provides antecedents for pronominal anaphora;

b. it provides the semantic type required by a clarification request;

c. it provides an attachment site for co-verbal gestures;

d. its content parts can be identified and addressed.

Recall from section 1 that the Reprise Content Hypothesis provides a stronger claim than Fregean compositionality: more complex contents are not just systematically combined from their parts, but the contributions from the parts have to be traceable within the complex content. This we achieve in virture of the feature CONSTITS mentioned above, whereas potential clarifiability arises from the update rule **parameter identification**, formulated above as (20)

The "QNP anatomy" (a phrase due to Cooper, 2013a), which will be an important basis for satisfying these desiderata, is based on a set triplet:

(24)
$$\begin{bmatrix} \text{q-params} : \begin{bmatrix} \text{refset} & : \textit{Set(Ind)} \\ \text{compset} & : \textit{Set(Ind)} \\ \text{maxset} & : \textit{Set(Ind)} \\ \text{c1} & : \overrightarrow{\textit{PType}}(\text{maxset}) \\ \text{c2} & : \text{union(maxset,refset,compset)} \end{bmatrix} \\ \text{q-cond} : \textit{Rel}(|\text{q-params.refset}|, |\text{q-params.compset}|) \end{bmatrix}$$

The arrow indicates a plural predicate type (*PType*), that is, a predicate that expects a set-valued argument. Condition c2 simply states that refset and compset add up to the maxset. The value of condition c1 is donated by the head noun and distributed over all maxset members (and thereby over refset and compset). The quantificational workhorse is the quantifier condition "q-cond": it captures what can be called the descriptive meaning of a QNP. For instance, the q-cond of *most* states that the refset is larger than the compset ($|\text{refset}| > |\text{compset}|$). Hence, q-cond not only expresses NP-internal quantification (i.e., quantification without a scope set from the VP), it also implements quantifiers as "sieves", a metaphor due to Barwise and Cooper (1981).

Singular is seen as a special case of plural which just adds the following constraint:

(25)
$$\begin{bmatrix} \text{q-params} : \begin{bmatrix} \text{refind} : \textit{Ind} \\ \text{c3} \quad : \text{in(refind, refset)} \end{bmatrix} \end{bmatrix}$$

RTT involves a twist in predication: the compset gives rise to "two-headed" propositions. For example, the propositional structure for the simple sentence *Most squirrels sleep* is given in (26), where sit-type is of type *RecType*:

(26)
$$\begin{bmatrix} \text{sit}{=}s_1 : \textit{Rec} \\ \text{sit-type}{=} \begin{bmatrix} \text{q-params} : \begin{bmatrix} \text{maxset} & : \textit{Set(Ind)} \\ \text{refset} & : \textit{Set(Ind)} \\ \text{compset} & : \textit{Set(Ind)} \\ \text{c0} & : \overrightarrow{\text{squirrel}}(\text{maxset}) \\ \text{c1} & : \text{union(maxset,refset,compset)} \end{bmatrix} \\ \text{q-cond} \;: |\text{q-params.refset}| > |\text{q-params.compset}| \\ \text{nucl} \;: \overrightarrow{\text{sleep}}(\text{q-params.refset}) \\ \text{anti-nucl} : \neg\overrightarrow{\text{sleep}}(\text{q-params.compset}) \end{bmatrix} \end{bmatrix}$$

Hence, there are several ways to form a propositional abstract from RTT propositions—namely over refset, compset, or refind. Two remarks are in order:

- Since refind is a special case of refset, we do not distinguish those cases and subsume refind to refset abstractions.
- In principle, the refset/compset distinction allows us to semantically distinguish positive and negative WhPs: positive ones ("Who PRED?") target the refset, negative ones ("Who does not" PRED?) can be seen to target the compset of the situational abstract of the question. However, in line with the distinction of negative and positive propositions in TTR-KoS, we treat negative questions as involving a negated nucl (and a double negated (equivalent but distinct from positive) anti-nucl).

The basic contribution of a *wh*-phrase to an interrogative meaning is the domain from which a propositional function will be constructed. It is this domain clarification for which can be sought. Hence, we add additional structure in *abstr* with a label *wh-dom*, which also gets projected as the dgb-params.x value of that sub-utterance.[7] Hence, the basic "anatomy" of WhP meaning in RTT is: The situation types of propositions on the RTT account factor out referential parameters in terms of q-params—see (24) and (26). Hence, questions and answers are constructed in terms of these parameter sets.

(27)
$$\begin{bmatrix} \text{wh-dom} = \begin{bmatrix}\text{refset} : \textit{Set(Ind)} \\ \text{c1} \;\; : \overrightarrow{\textit{PType}}(\text{refset})\end{bmatrix} : \textit{RecType} \\ \text{cont} : \begin{bmatrix}\text{x} = \text{wh-dom.refset}\end{bmatrix} \\ \text{dgb-params} : \begin{bmatrix}\text{x} = \text{wh-dom} : \textit{RecType}\end{bmatrix}\end{bmatrix}$$

A question's abstr now works as follow:

(28)
$$\begin{bmatrix} \text{s} = r_1 \\ \text{abstr} = f : T_1(T_2.\text{sit-type.q-params.refset}) \end{bmatrix}$$

which yields contents as in (29):

(29) a. *Who sleeps?* $\mapsto$
$$\begin{bmatrix} \text{sit} = r : \textit{Rec} \\ \text{abstr} = \begin{bmatrix} \text{wh-dom} = \begin{bmatrix}\text{refset} : \textit{Set(Ind)} \\ \text{c1} \;\; : \overrightarrow{\text{person}}(\text{refset})\end{bmatrix} : \textit{RecType} \\ f = \text{wh-dom}(\begin{bmatrix}\text{refset}{=}r.\text{refset} : \textit{Set(Ind)} \\ \text{nucl} : \overrightarrow{\text{sleep}}(\text{refset})\end{bmatrix}) \end{bmatrix} \end{bmatrix}$$

b. *Who does not sleep?* $\mapsto$
$$\begin{bmatrix} \text{sit} = r : \textit{Rec} \\ \text{abstr} = \begin{bmatrix} \text{wh-dom} = \begin{bmatrix}\text{refset} : \textit{Set(Ind)} \\ \text{c1} \;\; : \overrightarrow{\text{person}}(\text{refset})\end{bmatrix} : \textit{RecType} \\ f = \text{wh-dom}(\begin{bmatrix}\text{refset}{=}r.\text{refset} : \textit{Set(Ind)} \\ \text{nucl} : \neg\overrightarrow{\text{sleep}}(\text{refset})\end{bmatrix}) \end{bmatrix} \end{bmatrix}$$

Note that refset abstraction accommodates both singular and plural answers. Note further that the compset provides a straightforward link for maintaining situational identity between questions and answers in case of negative answers. For instance, answering "Who sleeps?" with "Not the squirrel" can be straightforwardly understood in an Austinian manner as being about the same situation since the NP negation indicates compset membership (cf. Lücking and Ginzburg, 2019).

- SimpleAns(p?) =
$$\left\{ \begin{bmatrix}\text{sit} = \text{s0} \\ \text{sit-type} = \begin{bmatrix}\text{nucl} : p\end{bmatrix}\end{bmatrix}, \begin{bmatrix}\text{sit} = \text{s0} \\ \text{sit-type} = \begin{bmatrix}\text{nucl} : \neg p\end{bmatrix}\end{bmatrix} \right\}$$
- SimpleAns($\lambda x.P(x)$) =
$$\left\{ \begin{array}{l} \begin{bmatrix}\text{sit} = \text{s1} \\ \text{sit-type} = \begin{bmatrix}\text{nucl} & : \text{P(s1.refset)} \\ \text{anti-nucl} & : \neg\text{P(s1.compset)}\end{bmatrix}\end{bmatrix}, \\ \begin{bmatrix}\text{sit} = \text{s2} \\ \text{sit-type} = \begin{bmatrix}\text{nucl} & : \text{P(s2.refset)} \\ \text{anti-nucl} & : \neg\text{P(s2.compset)}\end{bmatrix}\end{bmatrix}, \\ \ldots \end{array} \right\}$$
SimpleAns(p?) is answer to polar question ("whether Bill is running?" "No, he's not"/"Bill is not running"), SimpleAns($\lambda x.P(x)$) involves *Not NP* ("Who is running?" "Not Bill").
- AtomAnsRTT = answer given in terms of nucl
- NegAtomAnsRTT = answer given in terms of anti-nucl
- StrongExhaustiveAns = $\bigwedge\{\text{AtomAnsRTT}, \text{NegAtomAnsRTT}\}$ (i.e., an answer that enumerates all refset and compset members)

4 Accounting for the data

4.1 Putting together *wh*-meanings

In order to develop our account we need to appeal to a grammar for interrogatives. We assume the HPSG-TTR grammar developed in (Ginzburg

[7] We think that a similar account can be developed for intensional argument roles used with QNPs. Such cases are analyzed in RTT, following (Cooper, 2005), as the verb composing with a QNP's type value. Hence all that is required is to ensure also that this value is projected as the dgb-params.x value.

and Sag, 2000) and refined in (Ginzburg, 2012; Lücking et al., 2021). We start by exemplifying three constructions: sentential *wh*-interrogatives and two types of non-sentential *wh*-interrogatives ('sluicing'), one direct and the other used for clarification questions. In the case of sentential *wh*-interrogatives the filler daughter (specified as having a non-empty value for the feature *wh*) contributes the domain for the question; the range is identified with the content of the head daughter, with a substitution of filler daughter variable for gap variable. In the case of direct sluicing content is composed in an analogous way, save for the fact that the queried proposition is supplied by context—it is the nucleus of a quantified proposition that constitutes MaxQUD—and the substitution is the sluice WhP daughter for the focus establishing constituent variable: see Figure 3 (i) and (ii).[8] Finally for reprise sluicing (as well as other uses (Ginzburg, 2012, p. 258)), it allows a bare *wh*-phrase to denote MaxQUD given that the domain of the *wh*-phrase is the same as the domain of MaxQUD: see Figure 3 (iii).

4.2 Clarificational potential

The clarificational potential of *wh*-phrases is captured since the dgb-params.x value of the wh-phrase is the type specified by the label *wh-dom*; since the value specified is a type rather than an individual, there is no possibility of responding to such a clarification question with a witness (set).

4.3 Anaphoric potential

The anaphoric potential of *wh*-phrases in questions is subtle and requires a more detailed discussion, not least of the data, than we can offer here. All NPs provide antecedents via their content.x value. Intrasententially this is available subject to certain binding theory constraints. For discourse anaphora, available antecedents are sub-utterances in *active* moves (Ginzburg, 2012, p. 335) (essentially moves which address QUD or are PENDING). The restricted possibilities of wh-phrases and QNPs in intensional argument roles are due to a basic *horror vacui*, meaning that they avoid empty antecedent denotations, hence the need for accommodation in such cases. The basic idea we sketch for the wh-phrase case is this: via the accommodation rule in (30) (Ginzburg, 1997), the querier increments her *Topical* FACTS with a positive resolution of the *wh*-question;[9] this in turn provides an antecedent for the anaphor.

(30) Positive Resolution Accommodation

$$\begin{bmatrix} \text{pre} : \begin{bmatrix} \text{QUD} = \left\langle \text{q}, \text{Q} \right\rangle : \textit{poset(Question)} \\ \text{f} : \textit{Prop} \\ \text{c1} : \bigvee \textit{AtomAns}(\text{q}) \sqsubseteq \text{f} \end{bmatrix} \\ \text{effects} : \begin{bmatrix} \text{TOPICAL-FACTS} := \text{TOPICAL-FACTS} \cup \left\{ \text{f} \right\} \end{bmatrix} \end{bmatrix}$$

4.4 Incrementality

Following Ginzburg et al. (2020), QUD gets modified *incrementally*, that is, at a word-by-word latency. Technically, this is implemented by adopting the predictive principle of incremental interpretation in (31). This says that if one projects that the currently pending utterance (the preconditions in (31)) will continue in a certain way (pending.proj in (31)), then one can actually use this prediction to update one's DGB, concretely to update LatestMove with the projected move; this will, in turn, by application of the existing conversational rules, trigger an update of QUD:

(31) *Utterance Projection* :=

$$\begin{bmatrix} \text{preconds} : \begin{bmatrix} \text{pending.sit-type.proj} = \text{a} : \textit{Type} \end{bmatrix} \\ \text{effects} : \begin{bmatrix} \text{e1} : \textit{Sign} \\ \text{LatestMove} = \begin{bmatrix} \text{sit} = \text{e1} \\ \text{sit-type} = \text{a} \end{bmatrix} : \textit{LocProp} \end{bmatrix} \end{bmatrix}$$

Our proposed treatment of interrogative *clauses* in conjunction with our treatment of interrogative sluices is quasi–incremental (Schlesewsky and Bornkessel, 2004). That is, it allows to explain why an interrogative clause can already be (partially) understood as soon as the *wh*-phrase is uttered—there is already at that point an initial specification of a propositional function, namely its domain. More specifically, after processing '*wh*-phrase ... ', one can postulate a content where the projected but as yet unuttered constituent $u1$ contributes its content in an existentially quantified form, as in (6c), with a content as in (32a). Equally, this can give rise to a clarification request concerning the initial *wh*-phrase, as in (6d).

[8] 'fec' (focus establishing constituent) is the antecedent utterance whose scope builds up MaxQUD—in the case of sluicing it is the quantified NP in the antecedent utterance.

[9] Topical FACTS are, roughly, those facts that are *About* some question currently in QUD; see (Ginzburg, 2012, pp. 311–313). These play a role somewhat analogous to the right frontier constraint in discourse-tree based theories such as SDRT (Hunter et al., 2015).

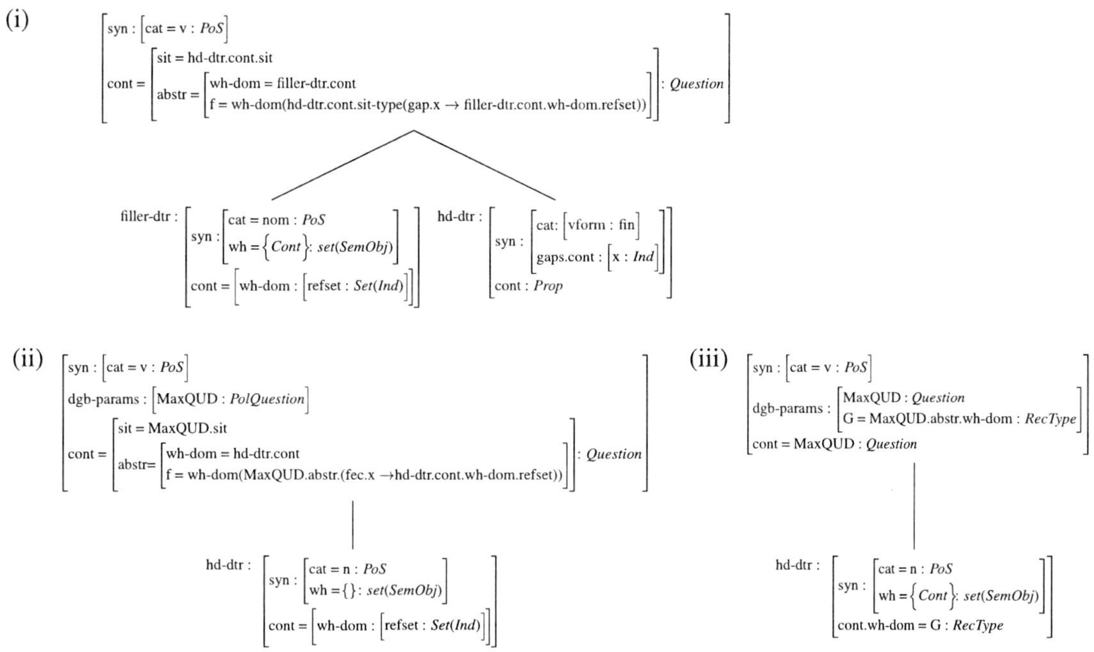

Figure 3: (i) Head-Filler Construction, for *ex situ wh*-sentences such as (2c.A): *Who should we contact __ for help?*, (ii) Sluice clause, for elliptical, non-reprise *wh*-questions such as A: A student left. B: *Who?* (iii) *wh*-anaphoric clause, for reprise or "echo" *wh*-phrases such as Fig. 1: *Who?*

(32)
$$\begin{bmatrix} \text{p} : \textit{Prop} \\ \text{q} = \begin{bmatrix} \text{sit} = \text{r} \\ \text{abstr} = \begin{bmatrix} \text{wh-dom} = \begin{bmatrix} \text{refset=r.refset} : \textit{Set(Ind)} \\ \text{c1} : \overrightarrow{\textit{person}}(\text{refset}) \end{bmatrix} \\ f = \text{wh-dom(p.sit-type)} \end{bmatrix} \end{bmatrix} : \textit{Question} \end{bmatrix}$$

4.5 The Harden example

Finally, we return to the example from Figure 1. This involves an initial utterance or gesture directed at James Harden. Using *parameter identification* targeting the addressee contextual–parameter, this leads to a context in which a reprise sluice (Figure 5) can be used, giving rise to the reading 'Who do you mean by this pointing gesture?'.

5 Summary and conclusions

In this paper we have sketched an extension of a recent theory of quantification to *wh*-phrases and questions. We have applied this account to several dialogical phenomena which we believe have not been addressed in previous work.

Acknowledgments

We thank the InqBnB referees for helpful comments and Robin Cooper for a useful discussion. This work is supported by a public grant overseen by the French National Research Agency (ANR) as part of the program 'Investissements d'Avenir' (reference: ANR-10-LABX-0083). It contributes to the IdEx Université Paris Cité - ANR-18-IDEX-0001.

References

Kazimierz Ajdukiewicz. 1926. Analiza semantyczna zdania pytajnego. *Ruch Filozoficzny*, 10:194b–195b.

John L. Austin. 1961. Truth. In James Urmson and Geoffrey J. Warnock, editors, *Philosophical Papers*. Oxford University Press. Paper originally published in 1950.

Jon Barwise and Robin Cooper. 1981. Generalized quantifiers in natural language. *Linguistics and Philosophy*, 4(2):159–219.

Jon Barwise and John Etchemendy. 1987. *The Liar*. Oxford University Press, New York.

Robin Cooper. 2005. Austinian truth, attitudes and type theory. *Research on Language and Computation*, 3(4):333–362.

Robin Cooper. 2013a. Clarification and generalized quantifiers. *Dialogue and Discourse*, 4:1–25.

Robin Cooper. 2013b. Update conditions and intensionality in a type-theoretic approach to dialogue semantics. *Proceedings of DamDial (SemDial 2013)*, pages 15–24.

Robin Cooper. 2023. *From Perception to Communication: a Theory of Types for Action and Meaning*. Oxford University Press.

Robin Cooper and Jonathan Ginzburg. 2015. Type theory with records for natural language semantics. In *Handbook of Contemporary Semantic Theory, second edition*, Oxford. Blackwell.

Jonathan Ginzburg. 1997. On some semantic consequences of turn taking. In *Proc. of the Munich Workshop on Formal Semantics and Pragmatics of Dialogue. University of Munich.*

Jonathan Ginzburg. 2012. *The Interactive Stance: Meaning for Conversation*. Oxford University Press, Oxford.

Jonathan Ginzburg and Robin Cooper. 2004. Clarification, ellipsis, and the nature of contextual updates. *Linguistics and Philosophy*, 27(3):297–366.

Jonathan Ginzburg, Robin Cooper, and Tim Fernando. 2014. Propositions, questions, and adjectives: a rich type theoretic approach. In *Proceedings of the EACL 2014 Workshop on Type Theory and Natural Language Semantics (TTNLS)*, pages 89–96, Gothenburg, Sweden. Association for Computational Linguistics.

Jonathan Ginzburg, Robin Cooper, Julian Hough, and David Schlangen. 2020. Incrementality and HPSG: Why not. In *Constraint-Based Syntax and Semantics: Papers in Honor of Danièle Godard*. CSLI Publications.

Jonathan Ginzburg and Ivan A. Sag. 2000. *Interrogative Investigations: the form, meaning and use of English Interrogatives*. Number 123 in CSLI Lecture Notes. CSLI Publications, Stanford: California.

Jonathan Ginzburg, Zulipiye Yusupujiang, Chuyuan Li, Kexin Ren, Aleksandra Kucharska, and Pawel Lupkowski. 2022. Characterizing the response space of questions: data and theory. *Dialogue & Discourse*, 13(2):79–132.

Pim Hopmans. 2019. Incrementally interpreting wh-questions using typelogical grammars. Master's thesis, Utrecht University.

Julie Hunter, Nicholas Asher, Eric Kow, Jérémy Perret, and Stergos Afantenos. 2015. Defining the right frontier in multi-party dialogue. In *19th Workshop on the semantics and pragmatics of dialogue (SemDial 2015-goDIAL)*, pages pp–95.

Lauri Karttunen. 1977. Syntax and semantics of questions. *Linguistics and Philosophy*, 1:3–44.

Manfred Krifka. 2001. For a structured meaning account of questions and answers. *Audiatur Vox Sapientia. A Festschrift for Arnim von Stechow*, 52:287–319.

Tadeusz Kubinski. 1960. An essay in the logic of questions. In *Proceedings of the XIIth International Congress of Philosophy (Venetia 1958)*, volume 5, pages 315–322, Firenze. La Nuova Italia Editrice.

Andy Lücking and Jonathan Ginzburg. 2019. Not few but all quantifiers can be negated: Towards a referentially transparent semantics of quantified noun phrases. In *Proceedings of the Amsterdam Colloquium 2019*, pages 269–278.

Andy Lücking and Jonathan Ginzburg. 2022. Referential transparency as the proper treatment of quantification. *Semantics and Pragmatics*, 15.

Andy Lücking, Jonathan Ginzburg, and Robin Cooper. 2021. Grammar in dialogue. In Stefan Müller, Anne Abeillé, Robert Borsley, and Jean-Pierre Koenig, editors, *Head-Driven Phrase Structure Grammar: The handbook*. Language Science Press.

Vedrana Mihaliček and Carl Pollard. 2012. Distinguishing phenogrammar from tectogrammar simplifies the analysis of interrogatives. In *Formal Grammar: 15th and 16th International Conferences, FG 2010, Copenhagen, Denmark, August 2010, FG 2011, Ljubljana, Slovenia, August 2011, Revised Selected Papers*, pages 130–145. Springer.

Matthew Purver. 2004. *The Theory and Use of Clarification in Dialogue*. Ph.D. thesis, King's College, London.

Matthew Purver and Jonathan Ginzburg. 2004. Clarifying noun phrase semantics. *Journal of Semantics*, 21:3:283–339.

Matthias Schlesewsky and Ina Bornkessel. 2004. On incremental interpretation: Degrees of meaning accessed during sentence comprehension. *Lingua*, 114(9).

Thomas P Urbach, Katherine A DeLong, and Marta Kutas. 2015. Quantifiers are incrementally interpreted in context, more than less. *Journal of memory and language*, 83:79–96.

Willemien Katrien Vermaat. 2006. *The Logic of Variation: A cross-linguistic account of wh-question formation*. 121. Landelijke Onderzoekschool Taalwetenschap.

Yimei Xiang. 2021. A hybrid categorial approach to question composition. *Linguistics and Philosophy*, 44(3):587–647.

Uninquisitive questions

Tom Roberts
University of Amsterdam
t.roberts@uva.nl

Abstract

The sort of denotation a sentence is assigned is typically motivated by assumptions about the discourse function of sentences of that kind. For example, the notion that utterances which are *functionally* inquisitive (asking a question) suggest denotations which are *semantically* inquisitive (expressing the multiple licit responses to that question) is the cornerstone of interrogative meaning in frameworks like Alternative Semantics (Hamblin, 1973) and Inquisitive Semantics (Ciardelli et al., 2018).

This paper argues that at least some kinds of questions systematically do not involve utterances with inquisitive content, based on novel observations of the Estonian discourse particle *ega*. Though *ega* is often labeled a 'question particle', it is used in both assertions and questions with sharply divergent discourse effects. I suggest that the relevant difference between assertive and questioning uses of *ega* is not semantic or sentence type-related, but rather reflects an interaction between a unified semantics for declaratives *ega*-sentences and different contexts of use. I then show that if we assume that *ega* presupposes that some aspect of the discourse context implicates the negation of *ega*'s prejacent, and that it occurs only in declarative sentences, we can derive its interpretation across a range of contexts: with the right combination of ingredients, we can ask questions with semantically uninquisitive sentences.

1 Introduction

A fundamental question in Inquisitive Semantics (Ciardelli et al., 2018) is what sorts of linguistic items generate semantic inquisitivity, in the sense of raising multiple mutually non-entailing alternatives. Polar interrogative clauses, for example, are a paradigmatic example of an inquisitive object, characterized by an inquisitive operator INT which is responsible for contributing inquisitivity, reminiscent of influential analyses of questions as denoting sets of answers to those questions (e.g. Hamblin, 1973; Karttunen, 1977; Groenendijk and Stokhof, 1982).

How can we tell what linguistic objects are inquisitive? In the case of interrogatives, their characteristic inquisitivity correlates with the fact that they canonically raise issues with multiple possible resolutions. This can be formally cashed out in various ways. For example, Farkas and Roelofsen (2017) propose a general-purpose utterance function that applies equally to both declaratives and interrogatives; the 'questioning' effect of interrogatives comes from an interaction between their inquisitive denotation and this utterance function. The difference between declaratives and interrogatives in this view comes from the assumption that declarative sentences denote a singleton set of propositions, and therefore raise issues with only a single maximal resolution.

But we cannot always straightforwardly link inquisitive denotations to inquisitive speech act functions. For instance, English rising declaratives (*You're in London?*) seem to ask questions, despite their declarative form. This pragmatic observation has motivated analyses of rising declaratives as having a (possibly compositionally determined) inquisitive denotation à la interrogatives (Roelofsen and Farkas, 2015; Farkas and Roelofsen, 2017; Jeong, 2018), but many others aim to derive their question-asking pragmatic function from the interaction between non-inquisitive declarative semantics *per se* and rising intonation (Truckenbrodt, 2006; Gunlogson, 2008; Krifka, 2015; Malamud and Stephenson, 2015; Westera, 2017, 2018; Rudin, 2022, to name but a few).

Whatever the right analysis of rising declaratives is, they raise the much larger issue of what path(s) languages make use of to get from denotations to pragmatic functions. To put a finer point on it: Do question-y pragmatics point to inquisitive

Proceedings of the 4th Workshop on Inquisitiveness Below and Beyond the Sentence Boundary (InqBnB4), pages 21–30
June 20, 2023.

denotations, or can pragmatic 'inquisitivity' arise via other means? And if the latter is true, what are those means?

This paper aims to shed light on the sentential denotation-speech act mapping through the lens of the Estonian left-periphery discourse particle *ega*. *Ega* is an interesting case from this perspective because it occurs in both questions (1) and assertions (2), but makes sharply different interpretive contributions in each case.[1] Also strikingly, *ega* only occurs in sentences with sentential negation (with some rare exceptions, see §4).

(1) *Context: Discussion diagnosing warning lights on a car dashboard*

Ega see pilt punasest kollaseks ei vahetu?
EGA this picture red.ELA yellow.TRA NEG change.NEG
'Does the icon not change from red to yellow?' (etTenTen 2021)[2]

(2) *Context: Speaker is sure that Russia would advance in the tournament, but they lost. They describe their reaction to this state of affairs:*

Ega ma eriti kurb ei olnud.
EGA I especially sad NEG was.neg
'I wasn't especially sad.' (etTenTen)

In questions, *ega* conveys a 'checking' function similar to tag questions, though it also is used in polite requests. By contrast, in assertions, *ega* offers a sense of 'epistemic reinforcement' that its prejacent is true, in contrast to some prior assumption. Despite this apparent duality of function, much more attention has been paid to the former use of *ega*, and it is often explicitly described in both formal and descriptive work as a 'negative question particle' (e.g. Metslang, 1981, 2017; Erelt et al., 1995).

The two guises of *ega* seem to be at odds with one another: *Ega*-assertions convey epistemic certainty, but *ega*-questions solicit addressee responses in a similar manner to interrogatives. We could reconcile these facts by assuming that there are two distinct versions of *ega* in the lexicon, one for declaratives, and one for interrogatives. This approach might well be sufficient for a description of *ega*'s discourse effects in various contexts, but it also leaves any similarities between the two completely accidental, such as their tendency to occur alongside sentential negation.

In this paper, I propose a different approach: we have the same *ega* in both questions and assertions, but its divergent behavior arises from interactions between this unified meaning and general pragmatic principles. I argue that *ega*-sentences are never inquisitive in the formal sense—they do not denote non-singleton sets of propositions—but they do come with a presupposition that generates a pragmatic clash with their prejacent in most discourse contexts, giving the sense that the addressee in fact has an issue to resolve. In this way, the apparent 'inquisitivity' of *ega*-questions is epiphenomenal, adding to a body of literature which teases apart semantic and pragmatic inquisitivity, and suggesting that questions can be derived pragmatically from the interaction between uninquisitive building blocks.

2 A profile of *ega*

I will first lay out the pragmatic profile of *ega* by describing its distribution. As mentioned, *ega* occurs almost exclusively in negative sentences, an observation I will revisit in §4. Here, 'negative' means marked by *sentential* negation, a combination of the negative particle *ei* and a special connegative form of the verb.[3] Thus, in this section, I will describe the three kinds of discourse functions *ega*-sentences of the form *ega not-p* may have.

2.1 *Ega* in questions

Canonically, *ega* occurs in two main types of questions. The first is polite requests, which can be naturally uttered in both informal and formal contexts, such as asking a stranger for directions or interacting with customer service over the phone. Generally, the speaker in these cases presents an obliging tone, similar to rough English paraphrases like *I don't suppose that...* or *Do you happen to...*:

(3) Ega sa ei oska öelda, kus asub Eesti Pank?
EGA you NEG can.NEG say where is.located Bank of Estonia
'I don't suppose you could tell me where the Bank of Estonia is?'

(4) Ega sul ratas ei ole?
EGA you.ADE bike NEG be.NEG

[1] In fact, *ega* has yet another life as a coordinating conjunction. I set this version of *ega* aside here.

[3] *Ei* can in fact be omitted in *ega*-sentences so long as the connegative verb is still present and thus the sentence is still identifiably negative-marked (Tamm, 2015).

'Do you happen to have a bike?'

The second class of *ega*-questions function like tentative assertions that $\neg p$, while additionally seeking confirmation from the addressee whether this is in fact the case (Metslang, 2017). This profile is reminiscent of tag questions (see e.g. Reese and Asher 2007).

(5) Ega jaanipäeva viktoriin liiga raske
EGA Midsummer.GEN quiz too difficult
ei olnud?
NEG was.NEG
'The quiz about Midsummer wasn't too difficult, right?' (Tamm 2015:411)

(6) Ega sa midagi pole unustanud?
EGA you anything be.NEG forgot.NEG
'You haven't forgotten anything, right?'
(Sign after airport security checkpoint)

While *ega*-questions of the confirmation sort are felicitous if the speaker seems to reasonably expect that p is false ((7) in Context 1), they are infelicitous if the addressee is neutral with respect to the truth or falsity of p (Context 2) or biased towards the truth of p (Context 3):

(7) *A doctor asking a patient a standardized series of questions to make a diagnosis:*

Ega sul ei ole valu seljas?
EGA you.ADE NEG be.NEG pain back.INE
'You don't have back pain, right?'
Context 1: Patient burned their hand on a stove. (7)✓
Context 2: Doctor has no information about patient's status. (7)#
Context 3: Patient fell off a ladder. (7)#

What both of these species of questions have in common is that the speaker presents themselves as committing (at least contingently) to $\neg p$, but solicit a response from the addressee to either agree with or refute $\neg p$.

2.2 *Ega* in assertions

In contrast with its questioning uses, *ega* has a life as an 'adversative' particle in assertions. Informally, it indicates that the speaker is committed to the truth of $\neg p$, in contrast with some existing evidence for p. As Keevallik and Habicht (2017) put it, *ega* 'challenges something that has been assumed by the prior speaker'. This assumption can come from many sources, including implicatures of previous speech acts (Keevallik, 2009) or even the addressee's (even non-linguistic) behavior (8).

(8) *A left dirty dishes in the sink and asks B to clean them. B responds:*

Ega ei ole sinu ema!
EGA NEG be.NEG your mother
'I'm not your mother!'

In (8), B is not challenging a literal assertion of motherhood, but rather the apparent implication of A's behavior. Importantly, however, *ega*-assertions are not licensed in cases of bald-faced disagreement, i.e. in responses to assertions of p itself (note that B's response in (9) is similarly infelicitous without the polarity particle *ei* 'no'):

(9) A: Ma võitsin mängu.
I won game
'I won the game.'
B: #Ei, ega sa ei võitnud!
no EGA you NEG win.PAST.NEG
'(No), you didn't win!'

2.3 Summary

Though *ega*-questions and *ega*-assertions differ fundamentally in whether they seem to be requesting information or providing it, both convey that the speaker believes $\neg p$ and that there is some reason to believe that p.

3 *Ega* as a context update modifier

In this section, I will motivate the central analytical claim of this paper: despite often being used to ask questions, *ega*-sentences are always declarative, and the interrogative uses are derived by means of a crucial interaction between the meaning of *ega* and its contexts of use. Throughout this section, I will only examine *ega*-sentences are always negative (that is, having the form *ega not-p*), since positive *ega*-sentences are rare; the polarity restriction itself will be addressed in §4.

3.1 *Ega*-questions are declarative

In order to obtain a unified analysis of *ega*, we must contend with the apparent heterogeneity of discourse functions of *ega*-claims. On the basis of the discourse effects of *ega*-questions, we might assume they are in fact interrogative clauses. However, there is good reason to believe that *ega*-questions are in fact declarative.

In terms of core sentence structure, declaratives and interrogatives are identical in Estonian; there is no obvious syntactic difference between a declarative and its corresponding polar interrogative, and there has been argued to be no reliable prosodic difference between them either (Keevallik, 2003; Asu, 2006; Salveste, 2015). Rather, neutral polar questions are typically characterized by adding a left-periphery particle *kas* to a corresponding vanila declarative.

(10) a. Liis on kodus.
Liis is home
'Liis is home.'

b. Kas Liis on kodus?
Q Liis is home
'Is Liis home?'

Absent a syntactic signature of clause type, we can only argue that *ega*-sentences are interrogative indirectly, but in fact, two additional pieces of evidence point toward a declarative analysis. First, as Keevallik (2009) points out, *ega* often co-occurs with epistemic particles that are incompatible with bonafide interrogatives, such as *vist* 'probably, I assume'. This is even the case in *ega*-sentences whose apparent discourse function is to request information (11):

(11) Ega sul ei köeta vist.
EGA you.ADE NEG heat.PASS.NEG probably
'I assume that your place is not heated?' (Keevallik 2009: 152)

Second, both *ega*-assertions and checking questions require the speaker to be biased toward the belief that $\neg p$ (as opposed to p), which is entirely unsurprising if *ega*-sentences are declaratives, since uttering a declarative sentence $\neg p$ (absent special intonation) typically commits the speaker to $\neg p$. We will revisit this notion in more detail below. It might seem at first glance that polite requests like (3) run counter to this line of reasoning, since the speaker in such cases clearly does not believe $\neg p$. I will propose that this is an artifact of the polite reasoning contexts: in fact, speakers of such *ega*-questions are presenting themselves as believing $\neg p$ for politeness reasons; I spell this out more concretely in §3.4.1.

I take these pieces of evidence to jointly tip the scales in favor of a declarative analysis of *ega*. One possible issue is that on their face, *ega*-sentences can be embedded under anti-rogative verbs—those which permit interrogative but not declarative complements—like *küsima* 'ask' and *uurima* 'investigate' in the following examples from blogs.

(12) Nancy isa küsib, et ega teil
Nancy.GEN father asks that EGA you.ADE
ju seal Eestis kartuleid et
after.all there Estonian.INE potatoes NEG
kasvatata.
grow.INF
'Nancy's father asks whether you really don't grow potatoes there in Estonia.'[4]

(13) Praamil tuleb kohe onu
ferry.ADE comes immediately uncle
kandikuga ja uurib, et ega sa
tray.COM and investigates that EGA you
teed ei taha.
tea NEG want.NEG
'On the ferry, the waiter comes right away with a tray and asks whether you would like some tea.'[5]

To my knowledge, *ega* occurs embedded under anti-rogative predicates only when those predicates have a quotative reading. For instance, (12) and (13) both exhibit obgliatory indexical shift: second person pronouns in the embedded clause refer to the addressee in the reported discourse context rather than the reader of the blog, characteristic of quoted, rather than indirectly reported, speech in Estonian (Teptiuk and Hirvonen, 2021). Thus, I follow Rudin (2019) in assuming that these are not instances of bonafide clause embedding, but rather mere quotation, in which *ega* is part of the reported speech (for ways of working this out more concretely, see a.o. Lahiri 2002 and Davidson 2015).

One final issue I will note is that if *ega*-sentences are declaratives, we might expect that they could be composed with *kas* to make a polar interrogative, but *ega* cannot co-occur with clausemate *kas* (14).

(14) *{Kas ega/ega kas} sul ratas ei
Q EGA/EGA Q you.ADE bike NEG
ole?
be.NEG
Intended: 'Don't you have a bicycle?'

I suggest that this is likely to be a fact about syntax—*kas* and *ega* both occur somewhere in the left periphery of a clause, above the canonical subject position and below the complementizer. If *kas* and *ega* are both competing for the same syntactic slot, their inability to co-occur is expected.[6]

[4] http://marikatom.blogspot.com/2010/05/uks-harilik-kartulivotu-paev.html

[5] Abridged from https://lillelaps.blogspot.com/2013/01/tsivilisatsioonide-kokkuporke-koht.html

[6] A reviewer points out that this competition story requires

3.2 *Ega* in the Table model

In assertive contexts, *ega* often serves the purpose of canceling an implicature, that is, *ega* $\neg p$ is uttered in contexts in which the addressee might have some 'good reason' in principle to believe p. We could equally characterize questioning uses of *ega* in a similar way, roughly that the addressee is presenting themselves as believing $\neg p$, despite such evidence, but additionally requiring some input from the addressee to settle the matter. I will treat the evidential requirement as the core contribution of *ega*:

(15) **Licensing conditions on *ega*, informal version**
Ega $\neg p$ is licensed iff there exists a body of evidence jointly available to the speaker and the addressee which could lead the addressee to form the belief that p.

To make my assumptions about components of discourse more precise, I adopt a version of the Table model of discourse Farkas and Bruce (2010). In a nutshell, the Table model distinguishes three main parts of utterance meaning: semantic denotation, the commitments it places upon speakers, and how the utterance guides potential futures of the conversation.

The Table model consists of four main components:

- A Stalnakerian **common ground** cg consisting of all propositions all discourse participants are publicly committed to, which describes a **context set** cs of all worlds compatible with cg ($cs = \bigcap cg$)
- The **Table**, a set of issues to be jointly resolved in the discourse[7]
- A set of **discourse commitments** DC_X for every discourse participant X consisting of propositions X has publicly committed to
- A **projected set** ps of possible common grounds enhanced by resolutions of the current QUD

In this model, discourses are assumed to be driven by a cooperative goal to shrink cs. This is achieved by making utterances which raise and resolving **issues**. Issues are sets of classical propositions (i.e., sets of sets of worlds), which are raised by being put on the Table, and resolved by a context set that entails one of its constituent propositions. Uttering a declarative sentence contributes an assertion, as follows:

(16) ASSERTION: Uttering a declarative sentence which expresses proposition p in context i yields an output context o s.t. (Farkas and Bruce 2010: Ex. 9)[8]
a. $T_o = T_i + \{p\}$
b. $DC_{Sp,o} = DC_{Sp,i} + p$
c. $ps_o = \{cg_i + p\}$
d. $c_o = c_i$ in all other respects

An assertion does three things: puts the singleton issue $\{p\}$ on the Table, commits the speaker to the truth of p, and adds an enhancement of the common ground with p to the projected set, intuitively specifying that the addressee should resolve the issue $\{p\}$ by adding p to the common ground.

I propose that uttering *ega not-p*, contributes the normal discourse effects of asserting $\neg p$ and additionally carries two presuppositions, contributed lexically by *ega*. I frame these presuppositions for the moment as licensing conditions on uttering negative *ega*-sentences rather than giving a lexical entry for *ega* itself due to complications about how *ega* interacts with polarity, which will be revisited in §4.

(17) **Licensing conditions on *ega*, final**
ega not-p can be uttered in context c iff:
a. $p \notin DC_{Ad}$
b. There is a body of evidence E accessible to Sp and Ad in c such that $E \models p$

The condition in (17a) states that it is not already common ground that the addressee believes p, which ensures that *ega* is not utterable in contexts where the addressee has asserted p themselves. and

the assumption that *kas* and *ega* both belong to the same syntactic category. This is not in principle a problem for the treatment of *ega*-sentences as uniformly declarative if *kas* is in a category which correlates to sentence type, as is commonly assumed for question particles cross-linguistically (see Bailey 2012), rather than interrogativity *per se*.

[7] In Farkas & Bruce's original formulation, the Table is a stack. In this paper I will only consider Tables which have only one issue on them at a time, so treating it as a set is adopted for simplicity.

[8] One could equally adopt the definition of assertion which assumes Inquisitive Semantics, i.e., that declarative sentences denote a singleton set of propositions, as in Farkas and Roelofsen (2017). Because I treat *ega*-sentences as uniformly uninquisitive, this complication is not necessary.

the condition in (17b) that the speaker believes that there is some contextually available evidence that entails that p. Taken together, *ega* expresses an estimation of the addressee's information state: it doesn't yet have p in it, but there is mutually available evidence that could lead them in that direction.

At this stage, the presupposition is still modeled somewhat informally. For the purposes of this paper, I will abstract away from how to model this presupposition more precisely, while acknowledging it raises interesting questions for future work; the important point of the subsequent analysis will be how this licensing condition at an intuitive level interacts with context.

3.3 *Ega*-assertions

Recall that in assertive cases, an *ega*-claim typically is taken to straightforwardly assert the prejacent, but indicates there was nevertheless reason to disbelieve that prejacent. Moreover, an *ega*-assertion is 'epistemically strong' as Keevallik (2009) puts it: it conveys a sense that the speaker is especially committed to the truth of $\neg p$. I propose that *ega*-sentences take on this assertive flavor when uttered in contexts in which the speaker has a greater **epistemic authority** with respect to p than the addressee, in the sense of Northrup 2014. Roughly, $AUTH_X(p)$ indicates the degree to which X is a reliable source about the truth (or falsity) of p:

(18) *Ega not-p* is interpreted as an assertion iff:
  a. $AUTH_{Sp}(p) > AUTH_{Ad}(p)$

A plain assertion of $\neg p$ commits the speaker to the truth of $\neg p$ with the reasonable assumption of the Gricean maxim of Quality, namely that people only assert propositions they believe to be true (Grice, 1975). The strengthening effect in *ega*-assertions comes from the contrast between a speaker's uttering $\neg p$ in a context in which they are a greater authority on it than the addressee—performing a canonical assertion—and *ega*'s presupposition requiring the context to be such that there is good reason for the addressee to believe p.

In other words, the speaker is demonstrating their commitment to $\neg p$ *despite evidence to the contrary*, and *ega* explicitly signals to the addressee not to be fooled by the evidence for p. This tension naturally gives rise to the sense that *ega*-assertions are especially forceful: a sincere assertion of $\neg p$ in the fact of evidence for p requires the speaker to be so certain that they override any ambient evidence for p.

3.4 *Ega*-questions and addressee authority

Unlike *ega*-assertions, *ega*-questions seem to solicit information from the addressee. While the two types of *ega*-questions (polite requests and checking questions) seem nevertheless distinct on the surface, they have a common core in that they both suggest that the speaker is a lesser epistemic authority on p than the addressee. If the speaker is unlikely to believe $\neg p$, we get the polite request reading; if the speaker is likely to believe $\neg p$, we get the checking reading.

3.4.1 Polite requests

One prototypical use of *ega*-questions is to make a polite request of the addressee. Given our declarative semantics, and the assumption that uttering declarative sentences adds their propositional content to the speaker's discourse commitment, this might seem an odd function. I propose that it can be understood by considering the interaction between the semantics of *ega* and general constraints on *politeness*. Consider (19):

(19) Context: Telephone call to an information line.

Ega te ei oska öelda Võru
EGA you.PL NEG can.NEG say Võru.GEN
bussijaama telefoninumbrit?
bus station.GEN phone number.PRT
'I don't suppose you can tell me the phone number of the Võru bus station?'
(Keevallik and Habicht 2017: ex. 33)

Polite request interpretations of *ega* arise when it is common ground both that the speaker believes p, and that the speaker believes that the addressee has greater authority than them with respect to the truth of p:

(20) *Ega not-p* is interpreted as a polite request iff:
  a. $B_{sp}(p)$
  b. $AUTH_{Sp}(p) < AUTH_{Ad}(p)$

The story goes like this: the speaker presents herself as committing to $\neg p$—in (19), that the addressee cannot provide the bus station's phone number. In this particular discourse context, it is implausible that the speaker actually believes $\neg p$, since they would not be calling otherwise. In the terms of Rudin (2022), the caller makes an INSINCERE (and thus pragmatically marked) discourse move by committing themselves to $\neg p$, while assuming that the addressee has evidence for p.

The act of making a commitment which is known to be insincere to all discourse participants can only be cooperative if being insincere is a way for the speaker to avoid committing a more egregious pragmatic violation, as in Optimality Theoretic approaches to pragmatics (e.g. Dekker and van Rooy, 2000).

In the case of *ega*, I propose that the competing pragmatic constraints at play are SINCERITY (committing oneself only to that which they believe to be true, Rudin 2022) and POLITENESS.[9] The idea is this: the presupposition of *ega* requires the caller in (19) to believe the addressee has good reason to believe they *can* report the number—in this case, the evidence being their job in a call center.

If we consider a plausible alternative utterance to (19) the speaker could have asked instead which is a bonafide interrogative (e.g. *What is the phone number of the bus station?*), such an utterance is preferable in terms of SINCERITY, since uttering an interrogative does not commit the speaker to any one particular answer to the question it denotes (Farkas and Bruce, 2010; Farkas and Roelofsen, 2017). However, the *ega*-request is more POLITE because it gives the addressee a chance to save face—maintain a positive social image—in the sense of Brown and Levinson (1987).

In Brown & Levinson's view, disagreeing with a preceding assertion is a face-threatening move. If the addressee has to decline the speaker's *ega*-request, itself socially undesirable, they can do so by *agreeing* with the speaker's presented commitment $\neg p$. In other words, the speaker sacrifices sincerity to mitigate the addressee's possible loss of face by letting them 'agree their way out' of a potentially face-endangering situation should they have to give the speaker an answer they don't want. If the addressee was asked directly for the phone number and couldn't provide it, they would incur a double-whammy of social violations: being unable to answer a question, and being unable to help the speaker. By saying an *ega*-sentence instead, the speaker presents themselves as believing the addressee can't help them, giving the addressee a way to decline the request while saving face.

Given a choice between being insincere and being impolite, then, the proposal is that speakers are opting for the former when they make a polite request using *ega*. (In OT terms, we could say that the goal of being POLITE *outranks* that of being SINCERE.)

3.4.2 Checking questions

Recall that checking *ega*-questions—requests for the addressee to validate the truth of $\neg p$— convey that the speaker is fairly sure that $\neg p$ is the case, but nevertheless wants some validation about this from the addressee. I formalize the felicity conditions as follows:

(21) *Ega not-p* is interpreted as a checking question iff:
   a. $\neg B_{sp}(p)$[10]
   b. $AUTH_{Sp}(p) < AUTH_{Ad}(p)$

Normally, making assertions in a context where the addressee is assumed to be a greater authority about the truth of the asserted proposition is infelicitous:

(22) #You're hungry. (Northrup 2014: ex. 129)

This can be again be attributed to the Gricean maxim of Quality: the speaker's evidence is not sufficient to make their claim. With *ega not-p*, the tension between apparently asserting $\neg p$ on one hand and presupposing evidence for p on the other poses a natural conflict that demands resolution. Uttering *ega not-p* emphasizes this mismatch. If the speaker is taken to be an authority on p, the addressee has no reason not to take them at their word that $\neg p$. But if the *addressee* is an assumed authority, highlighting the conflict between the speaker's epistemic state and contextual evidence can only serve the function of asking the addressee to make the call between them.

For instance, in the forum post in (23), the speaker follows up a question about whether it is potentially problematic to forget taking antidepressants with an *ega*-sentence about specific repercussions:

(23) Can constantly changing antidepressants and forgetting to take them have a negative

[9]This is of course a gross oversimplification, since politeness itself involves many competing constraints, but I leave the formulation fairly general here for purposes of space.

[10]Note that this condition requires merely that the speaker not believe p, rather than the stronger condition that they believe $\neg p$. I make this formal choice to allow for the fact that the speaker's bias for $\neg p$ might fall short of what we would want to call 'belief'. I assume that the fact that *ega* is incompatible with contexts where the speaker is neutral about p comes from the infelicity of asserting $\neg p$ in such a context.

effect?...

Ega sellest ei teki epsilepsiat või
EGA this NEG cause.NEG epilepsy or
šõsofreniat[sic]?
schizophrenia?
'This doesn't cause epilepsy or schizophrenia?' (etTenTen)

In this advice-seeking situation, the speaker puts forward $\neg p$ as their 'best guess' for what is true, while signaling to the addressee that they would like confirmation. Had they asserted $\neg p$ directly, they would have conveyed that there was no reason to believe otherwise than $\neg p$, a nakedly odd conversational move to make if the addressee knows more about the truth of p.

3.5 Analytical summary

In this section, I proposed that three kinds of *ega*-sentences—assertions, polite requests, and checking questions—arise from a unified denotation of such sentences being uttered in contexts with different configurations of speaker belief and relative authority between speaker and addressee.

In particular, the sense of *questioning* in the latter two cases arises from the use of *ega*-statements in contexts where the speaker has relatively low epistemic authority about the truth of the prejacent. In effect, *ega* serves to highlight a contrast between the assertion that $\neg p$ and some available evidence for p, and uttering it in contexts where the addressee is in a better position than the speaker to resolve this tension gives rise to the 'inquisitive' function of *ega*-questions.

4 Whence the polarity generalization

One outstanding issue given the analysis of *ega* thus far is its allergy to positive sentences:

(24) *Ega sul on valu seljas.
EGA you.ADE is pain back.INE
'You EGA have back pain.'[11]

After all, the intuitive characterization of *ega*-sentences is that they presuppose there was good reason to believe p, but this presupposition does not in and of itself derive the polarity restriction on *ega*-sentences.

To probe the polarity constraint, we must first make explicit what *ega* itself contributes to interpretation, rather than just its discourse effects in full utterances. There are two plausible logical forms for *ega*-sentences with negation if we treat *ega* as a propositional operator. One is that *ega* takes the prejacent $\neg p$ as an argument (*ega* $(\neg p)$)[12] and presuppose there is evidence for the negation of the argument, p. The other is that *ega* takes the positive prejacent as an argument, but occur itself within the scope of negation ($\neg$(*ega* p)), and presuppose that there is evidence for that argument p.

These LFs make different predictions for what *ega* should mean in non-negated contexts. If *ega* takes widest scope, we expect *ega p* to have an analogous reading to *ega not-p*: that is, *ega p* should **assert** p and presuppose evidence for $\neg p$. On the other hand, if *ega* scopes below negation, *ega* in a positive sentence should reinforce the alignment of the speaker's assertion that p with evidence for p.

In fact, *ega* does show up in positive sentences, albeit rarely (25). Such cases only exhibit the former reading, suggesting that *ega* takes wide scope:

(25) *A comment on a newspaper article about cat rabies with a picture of a cat claimed to be unrelated to the story:*

Ega see pildil olev kass on ka
EGA this picture.ADE be.PCP cat is also
kahtlase näoga...
suspicious face.COM
'In fact the cat in this picture looks suspicious too...'
(Keevallik and Habicht 2017, ex. 27)

The author of (25) asserts a positive p (*The cat has a suspicious face*), but indicates this is contrary to a contextually-supported assumption that the cat does not have rabies. Keevallik and Habicht (2017) take examples like (25) to indicate that *ega* in assertive contexts is not limited to negative sentences, and note that similar examples occur more commonly in spoken language.

But if *ega p* is in fact *possible*, we have a conundrum: why is it nevertheless so rare in non-negated contexts? Because the polarity restrictions on *ega* are not categorical, we don't want to derive its negative tendencies by all-or-nothing constraints, such as by stipulating that *ega* is a negative polarity item.

A full account of the polarity sensitivity of *ega* is outside the scope of this paper, but I suggest that the paucity of positive *ega*-sentences could be a

[11] I use an asterisk here to indicate systematic unacceptability rather than ungrammaticality *per se*.

[12] We might also think *ega* operates at the level of illocutionary force and instead takes an utterance or a sentence as an argument; for present purposes what matters is whether or not negation is inside whatever argument is fed to *ega*.

distributional artifact arising from an asymmetry in the pragmatics of uttering positive and negative declaratives.

It is a longstanding observation that negative assertions are pragmatically marked: uttering $\neg p$ often presupposes (in a weak, defeasible sense) that there was reason to believe that p or that p was under discussion, where uttering p has no analogous implications (Givón, 1978, et seq.). Given independently-motivated pressures to presuppose as much as possible (perhaps analogous to a principle like Maximize Presupposition, e.g. Heim 1991), we might expect that negative sentences are preferred utterances over logically equivalent positive sentences (e.g. *John is not married* vs. *John is a bachelor*) in contexts where there is evidence to believe that these sentences are false (i.e. that John is married).

Of course, *ega* itself also presupposes the existence of evidence which conflicts with a prejacent proposition, so the explanation could be that *ega* requires the exact kind of input contexts which would lead one to prefer a negative sentence over a positive alternative, so we expect the negative version to be used unless there is some special independent pressure to pick the positive alternative specifically, whatever this pressure might be. This story generates the testable hypothesis that positive *ega*-sentences are generally less acceptable than interpretively equivalent negative *ega*-sentences. For example, we might expect that (25) would be less acceptable in the same context than a similar version where the prejacent of *ega* is a negative proposition, e.g., *This cat isn't healthy*. I leave exploration of this hypothesis for future research.

5 Conclusion

A major project at the semantics-pragmatics interface is understanding the relation between the denotation of a sentence and the function of uttering that sentence in context. This paper brings new data from Estonian to bear on this task. I have argued that the discourse particle *ega*, despite having a seemingly expansive range of potential discourse effects, can receive a single unified denotation if we make sensible assumptions about the way its semantics interacts with contexts of use. The apparent 'inquisitivity' of *ega* in some contexts, rather than being a result of inherently inquisitive semantics, comes from the tension inherent in making assertions that presuppose there is evidence to the contrary in contexts where the addressee is better equipped to adjudicate between these conflicting sources.

The role that discourse particles have in determining discourse function remains a fertile ground for cross-linguistic exploration. Just as interrogative sentences can serve many different kinds of communicative functions besides just asking questions (Lauer and Condoravdi, 2012), there are likewise multiple pathways to generating questioning speech acts, and this paper represents an attempt to chart a new part of this underexplored terrain. A broader view of the typology of inquisitive pragmatics may help us get closer to understanding the ur-question: What *is* a question, anyway?

References

Eva Liina Asu. 2006. Rising intonation in Estonian: An analysis of map task dialogues and spontaneous conversations. In Reijo Aulanko, Leena Wahlberg, and Martti Vainio, editors, *Fonetiikan päivät 2006* [The Phonetics Symposium 2006], pages 1–8. Helsinki: Helsinki University.

Laura Bailey. 2012. *The Syntax of Question Particles*. Ph.D. thesis, Newcastle University.

Penelope Brown and Stephen C. Levinson. 1987. *Politeness: Some universals in language use*. Cambridge: Cambridge University Press.

Ivano Ciardelli, Jeroen Groenendijk, and Floris Roelofsen. 2018. *Inquisitive Semantics*. Oxford University Press.

Kathryn Davidson. 2015. Quotation, demonstration, and iconicity. *Linguistics and Philosophy*, 38:477–520.

Paul Dekker and Robert van Rooy. 2000. Bi-directional Optimality Theory: An Application of Game Theory. *Journal of Semantics*, 17(3):217–242.

Mati Erelt, Reet Kasik, Helle Metslang, Henno Rajandi, Kristiin Ross, Henn Saari, Kaja Tael, and Silve Vare. 1995. *Eesti Keele Grammatika II*. Tallinn: Eesti Teaduste Akadeemia Eeesti Keele Instituut.

Donka Farkas and Kim Bruce. 2010. On reacting to assertions and polar questions. *Journal of Semantics*, 27(1):81–118.

Donka Farkas and Floris Roelofsen. 2017. Division of Labor in the Interpretation of Declaratives and Interrogatives. *Journal of Semantics*, 34(2):237–289.

Talmy Givón. 1978. Negation in language: Pragmatics, function, ontology. In Peter Cole, editor, *Pragmatics*, Syntax and Semantics 9, pages 69–112. Academic Press, New York.

Paul Grice. 1975. Logic and Conversation. In P. Cole and J. Morgan, editors, *Syntax and Semantics 3: Speech Acts*. Leiden, The Netherlands: Brill.

Jeroen Groenendijk and Martin Stokhof. 1982. Semantic analysis of wh-complements. *Linguistics and Philosophy*, 5:117–233.

Christine Gunlogson. 2008. A question of commitment. *Belgian Journal of Linguistics*, 22:101–136.

Charles L. Hamblin. 1973. Questions in Montague English. *Foundations of Language*, 10(1):41–53.

Irene Heim. 1991. Artikel und definitheit [*Articles and definiteness*]. In A. von Stechow and D. Wunderlich, editors, *Semantik: Ein internationales Handbuch der zeitgenössischen Forschung*, pages 487–535. Berlin: de Gruyter.

Sunwoo Jeong. 2018. Intonation and sentence type conventions: Two types of rising declaratives. *Journal of Semantics*, 35(2):305–356.

Lauri Karttunen. 1977. Syntax and semantics of questions. *Linguistics and Philosophy*, 1(1):3–44.

Leelo Keevallik. 2003. Terminally Rising Pitch Contours of Response Tokens in Estonian. In *Crossroads of Language, Interaction, and Culture*, volume 5, pages 49–65.

Leelo Keevallik. 2009. The grammar-interaction interface of negative questions in Estonian. *SKY Journal of Linguistics*, 22:139–172.

Leelo Keevallik and Külli Habicht. 2017. Grammaticalization, (inter)subjectification, and sequencing of actions: the Estonian epistemic (question) particle *ega*. *Linguistica Uralica*, 53(2):81–105.

Manfred Krifka. 2015. Bias in commitment space semantics: Declarative questions, negated questions, and question tags. In Sarah D'Antonio, Mary Moroney, and Carol Rose Little, editors, *Proceedings of SALT 25*, pages 328–345.

Utpal Lahiri. 2002. *Questions and Answers in Embedded Contexts*. Oxford Studies in Theoretical Linguistics.

Sven Lauer and Cleo Condoravdi. 2012. The basic dynamic effect of interrogative utterances. Presentation at the 13th Text Linguistics Society Conference, University of Texas, Austin.

Sophia Malamud and Tamina Stephenson. 2015. Three ways to avoid commitment: Declarative force modifiers in the conversational scoreboard. *Journal of Semantics*, 32(2):275–311.

Helle Metslang. 1981. *Küsilause Eesti Keeles* [Interrogative sentences in Estonian]. Tallinn: Academy of Sciences of the Estonian SSR Institute of Language and Literature.

Helle Metslang. 2017. Kommunikatiivsed lausetüübid [*Communicative sentence types*]. In Mati Erelt and Helle Metslang, editors, *Eesti keele süntaks* (Eesti keele varamu 3), pages 515–532. Tartu: Tartu Ülikooli Kirjastus.

Oliver Northrup. 2014. *Grounds for Commitment*. Ph.D. thesis, UC Santa Cruz.

Brian Reese and Nicholas Asher. 2007. Prosody and the interpretation of tag questions. In Louise McNally and Estela Puig-Waldmüller, editors, *Proceedings of Sinn und Bedeutung 11*, pages 448–462.

Floris Roelofsen and Donka Farkas. 2015. Polarity particle responses as a window onto the interpretation of questions and assertions. *Language*, 91(2):359–414.

Deniz Rudin. 2019. Embedded rising declaratives and embedded quotation. In Katherine Blake, Forrest Davis, Kaelyn Lamp, and Joseph Rhyne, editors, *Proceedings of SALT 29*, pages 1–21.

Deniz Rudin. 2022. Intonational commitments. *Journal of Semantics*, 39(2):339–383.

Nele Salveste. 2015. *On the pragmatic and semantic functions of Estonian sentence prosody*. Ph.D. thesis, Ludwig-Maximilians-Universität München.

Anne Tamm. 2015. Negation in Estonian. In Matti Miestamo, Anne Tamm, and Beáta Wagner-Nagy, editors, *Negation in Uralic Languages*, pages 399–432. John Benjamins.

Denys Teptiuk and Johannes Hirvonen. 2021. Perspective shift in reported discourse of Finno-Ugric languages. Presentation at the Societas Linguistica Europaea.

Hubert Truckenbrodt. 2006. On the semantic motivation of syntactic verb movement to C in German. *Theoretical Linguistics*, 32(3):257–306.

Matthijs Westera. 2017. *Exhaustivity and intonation: A unified theory*. Ph.D. thesis, University of Amsterdam.

Matthijs Westera. 2018. Rising declaratives of the quality-suspending kind. *Glossa: A Journal of General Linguistics*, 3:1–32.

mage as a bias particle in interrogatives

Maryam Mohammadi
University of Konstanz
maryam.mohammadi@uni-konstanz.de

Abstract

This paper investigates Farsi particle *mage* in interrogatives, including both polar and constituent/Wh questions. I will show that *mage* requires both contextual evidence and speaker's prior belief in the sense that they contradict each other. While in polar questions (PQs) both types of bias can be straightforwardly expressed through the uttered proposition (cf. Mameni 2010), Wh-questions (WhQs) do not provide such a propositional object. To capture this difference, I propose *Answerhood* as the relevant notation that provides the necessary object source for *mage* (inspired by Theiler 2021). The proposal establishes the felicity conditions and the meaning of *mage* in relation to the (contextually) restricted answerhood in both polar and constituent questions.

1 Introduction

Discourse particles are useful tools for organizing conversations by fitting an utterance into the context. The small words (usually) do not contribute to the core propositional content but convey expressive meaning. They indicate information that would otherwise need to be described by the speaker or inferred by the addressee. Therefore, many studies investigate the intended meaning expressed by these particles, as well as the felicity conditions that capture the necessary properties of the discourse or the interlocutors.

Zimmermann (2011) introduces three semantic core functions for discourse particles (in German): **(i)** marking the expression as part of the Common Ground (e.g., *ja*), **(ii)** indicating that the expression is not activated with one of the discourse participants (e.g., *doch*), and **(iii)** weakening the commitment to the expression (e.g., *wohl*). More recently, Theiler (2021) provides examples of the particle *denn* being felicitous in WhQs but not in PQs, which could not be explained neither by the expressive meaning nor by the felicity conditions of *denn*. Theiler claims that for certain particles, such as *denn*, we also need to consider *which notion of semantic content* are linked to them. She argues that while discourse particles are usually relevant to the informativity notion in declaratives (modeled as a proposition), this notion becomes more tricky in questions that seek information. Following Roelofsen and Farkas (2015), she suggests highlighting as the relevant notion in questions. In her proposal, particle *denn* indicates that learning the highlighted proposition is a necessary precondition for the speaker to proceed the discourse.

Particle *mage* in Farsi seems to require a similar consideration. It is worth noting that *mage* literally means 'unless' in non-interrogatives (see Section 5 for some examples), however, this paper focuses only on its discursive function in interrogatives. Like many other discourse particles that have double lives (e.g., *ja* and *denn* in German Lindner 1991, Theiler 2021), I consider particle *mage* in interrogatives as a homonymous with the conditional *mage* in non-interrogatives. I leave the discussion about its conditional *mage* for future studies.

A comparison between minimal pairs of polar and constituent questions with and without *mage* reveals that the particle carries additional information about both speaker's prior belief and contextual evidence in the given context. Example (1) presents a canonical polar question in Farsi (in the form of a rising declarative), simply asking whether or not Ali came to the party (p?). Example (2), which asks the same question, not only signals the speaker's prior belief/expectation against the uttered proposition p, *that Ali didn't come* (Mameni, 2010), but also requires contextual evidence for p.

Proceedings of the 4th Workshop on Inquisitiveness Below and Beyond the Sentence Boundary (InqBnB4), pages 31–39

(1) Ali mehmuni umad?
Ali party came
'Did Ali come to the party?'

(2) mage Ali mehmuni umad?
MAGE Ali party came
'Did Ali come to the party?'

(3) ki mehmuni umad?
who party came
'Who did come to the party?'

(4) mage ki mehmuni umad?
MAGE who party came
'Who did come to the party?'

On the other hand, examples (3) and (4) are minimal pairs of WhQs in Farsi, both seeking the list of people at the party. While in PQs, the meaning of *mage*, as the speaker's contrary expectation, has been interpreted in relation to the uttered proposition, it cannot be reconstructed in WhQs as in (4). To understand the exact function of *mage* in WhQs, further discourse analysis is required.

In the next section, I will present examples of *mage* in PQs, arguing that it necessarily requires contextual evidence. Then, we will see examples of *mage* in WhQs, and I will demonstrate that *mage* perform the same function in both types of questions (with respect to their alternative set of answers). In Section 3, I propose a unified analysis based on the *answerhood* notation for the meaning of the discourse particle *mage* in both polar and constituent questions. Section 4 introduces further issues about *mage*. We will have a look at the previous studies about *mage* in Section 5. Finally, the conclusion will be presented in Section 6.

2 The Data

A large and growing body of literature has investigated the questions that require *original bias* (OB) as speaker's prior (epistemic) belief (Ladd 1981, Romero and Han 2004), or *contextual bias* (CB) as evidence mutually available to all participants in a conversation (Büring and Gunlogson 2000) or their combinations (Domaneschi et al. 2017).

Particle *mage*, which can appear in both positive and negative polar questions, expresses speaker's prior belief (OB) contrary to the uttered proposition in the question (cf. *really*-questions in Romero and Han 2004). In positive polar questions, such as in (5), the speaker has the prior belief that Ali didn't come to the party, while in negative polar questions like (6), it signals the reverse belief that Ali came.

(5) mage Ali mehmuni umad?
MAGE Ali party came
'Did Ali come to the party?'

(6) mage Ali mehmuni na-yumad?
MAGE Ali party NEG-came
'Did Ali not come to the party?'

Regarding the implication of the speaker's belief, Mameni (2010) shows that *mage* is felicitous in contexts that carry the speaker's prior expectation. Thus, since example (7) implicates that the speaker didn't expect Ali went to the party, it is truly predicted to be infelicitous (#) in Context 1 (as well as in out-of-the-blue contexts).

(7) A: mage Ali mehmuni umad?
MAGE Ali party came
'Did Ali come to the party?'

Context 1: A calls B to know about the guests who went to the party last night.

Context 1.1: ...A doesn't think that Ali went to the party.

✓ **Context 1.2:** ....B says that she had a nice conversation with Ali at the party. A didn't think Ali went to the party.

Although the OB is implemented in the continuation as in Context 1.1, it is still infelicitous (#). In other words, the suggested implicature (of the speaker's belief) is not enough to predict the infelicity of Context 1.1. When Context 1 is continued as in Context 1.2, it provides the proper setting (✓) for example (7). Therefore, the felicitous context for *mage* requires both CB and OB.

Furthermore, particle *mage* can be used in different WhQs as in examples (8)-(11) (the negative forms are omitted for brevity).

(8) mage ki umade?
MAGE who came
'MAGE who did come?'

(9) mage či xaridi?
MAGE what bought
'MAGE what did you buy?'

(10) mage koja rafti?
MAGE where went
'MAGE where did you go?'

(11) mage kei rafti?
MAGE when went
'MAGE when did you go?'

Let's focus on the first example with *ki* 'who' and find a felicitous context. In the given context in (12), *mage* indicates that the speaker did not expect any celebrities to be at the party and is now inquiring about which celebrities were there. That implies that although question (12) does not explicitly state a specific proposition as the speaker's belief, the context suggests that the speaker held a contrary belief regarding the restriction of the guests who were celebrities over all of the guests who went to the party.

(12) **Context:** A calls B to know about the guests who went to the party last night. B says that it was fun to see some celebrities there. A didn't expect that there were any celebrities at the party.

A: mage ki-â umadan?
MAGE who-PL came
'MAGE who did come?'

To figure out the meaning of *mage* in WhQs, we need to investigate the domain of the Wh-phrase, which is somehow restricted by *mage*. Assume that we have the following list of professors in context (13): {Valeria, Wolfgang, Xavier, Yara, and Zachary}, where only {Yara and Zachary} are the famous ones. Semantically, the same question *Who did you invite?* is asked in (A1) and (A2). Considering the context, both answers in (B1) and (B2) are acceptable in response to (A1), albeit with different preference order. However, only (B2) is the felicitous answer to (A2).

In other words, the speaker in (A1) would be looking for either all the invited professors or just the famous ones. Therefore, both (B1) and (B2) are felicitous responses, respectively. It is worth noting that prosody, such as an enthusiastic intonation, and/or expressives like *awesome*, could help guide the interpretation towards the contextually restricted set of famous professors rather than all guests. For instance, if speaker A expresses *âlie!* 'Awesome!' at the beginning of the question in (A1) and/or asks the question with an enthusiastic intonation, then (B2) is more likely to be the answer rather than (B1).

(13) A and B and C are the organizers of a conference. A wants to finalize the list of the invited guests.

A: Let's make a list. Who did you invite?

B: I invited some professors, two of them are so famous.

A1: ki-â ro davat kardi?
awesome who-PL ACC invite did?
'Who did you invite?'

A2: mage ki-â ro davat kardi?
MAGE who-PL ACC invite did?
'Who did you invite?'
⇝ The speaker didn't expect any famous professors.

B1: I invited Valeria, Wolfgang, Xavier, Yara and Zachary

B2: I invited Yara and Zachary

The question in (A2) implies that the speaker didn't expect any famous professors and further restricts the question to only the famous ones. Hence, if B starts listing all the invited professors as in (B1), speaker A would complain and explicitly mention that she meant which famous professors. Consequently, only (B2) is the appropriate answer to question (A2). It is important to note that any expressive term like *awesome* or prosody, whether usual or enthusiastic intonation, does not affect the acceptability of the answers to (A2). It is worth emphasizing that while both answers are somewhat acceptable in response to (A1), in the case of (A2), it is not a matter of answer preference but rather a matter of felicity.

Overall, the mandatory presence of contextual evidence in *mage* questions introduces a certain semantic object, which then becomes available as an anaphoric reference. The context restricts the question under discussion by narrowing down the alternative set of answers. More specifically, in *mage*-PQs, the uttered proposition in the question indicates the restriction over the contextual evidence. Similarly, the evidence in *mage*-WhQs obligatorily restricts the alternative set of answers to a subset list. In both types of questions, *mage* refers to the restricted set object, indicating that the speaker did not expect such a restriction. In the next section, I will propose an account based on the answerhood of the questions.

3 Proposal

The discursive function of *mage* in both polar and constituent questions can be formulated based on the *Answerhood* notation (instead of the uttered proposition in *mage*-PQs). According to the literature, the denotation of a question is a set of propositions that correspond to the possible answers (Hamblin 1973, Karttunen 1977). In the case of polar questions (PQs) (ϕ?), the denotation returns a binary set $\{\phi, \neg\phi\}$, including the positive and negative answers. On the other hand, for WhQs (wh_x P?), the denotation may generate multiple members $\{P(x)|x \in D_e\}$, where each member represents a possible answer to the question.

The alternative set of answers can be contextually restricted, meaning that the restricted set is a subset of all possible alternatives (cf. contextual variables in Martinez 2003). These (evidential) restrictions, particularly in WhQs, introduce specific semantic objects that can be referred to anaphorically using *mage* (cf. Theiler 2021). In this context, the restriction generates a proper subset from the alternative set. Based on this understanding, the denotation of *mage* can be formulated as follow:

(14) $[\![mage\ \phi?]\!] = [\![\phi?]\!]$, provided that there is a proper subset Q' of $[\![\phi?]\!]$ such that for all q in Q':
- q is supported by the contextual evidence, and
- the speaker did not expect q.

Following (14), the contextual evidence captures the discourse anaphoricity of *mage* to the subset answerhood, while the particle expresses that the speaker didn't expect such a restriction to hold. Now, let's go through the examples and see if the account can explain the data.

Starting with polar questions as in (7), which is repeated here in (15), the denotation of the question is the alternative set of answers, as shown in (a). The context implies *that Ali came*, as in (b). Regarding the (semantic) alternative set in (a) and the (contextually) restricted set in (b), the required proper subset condition is satisfied in (c) and (d), where *mage* indicates that the speaker didn't expect the restriction to hold.

(15) MAGE did Ali come?

a. $[\![$mage did Ali come?$]\!]=\{come(a), \neg come(a)\}$

b. Contextual Evidence for $\{come(a)\}$

c. $\{come(a)\} \subset \{come(a), \neg come(a)\}$, and

d. The speaker didn't expect that Ali came.

Moving on to WhQs as in example (13), repeated here in (16), the non-restricted set of alternatives results in a list of all invited professors, as shown in (a). However, the context suggests that there is a restricted list of famous invited professors, which narrows down the answerhood to a subset list, as illustrated in (b). In such cases, *mage* can felicitously appear since the subset condition is supported by the context in (c), and the particle signals that the speaker did not expect the restriction.

(16) MAGE who did you invite?

a. $[\![$mage who did you invite$]\!]$ = $\{invited(x) \mid Professor(x)\}$

b. Contextual Evidence for $Y = \{invited(y) \mid Professor(y) \wedge famous(y)\}$

c. Taking X the set in (a), $Y \subset X$

d. The speaker didn't expect any famous prof.

In summary, *mage* is felicitous in both polar questions with a binary set of alternatives, as well as in WhQs with a multiple member set, when the context indicates a restriction for a proper subset of the possible answers. In PQs, the evidence signals a single proposition, while in WhQs, it can result in a subset of multiple members. The contextual evidence provides the subset answerhood object, and particle *mage* implies that the speaker did not expect such restrictions to hold.

Lastly, it is worth noting that the proposal predicts that *mage* is not felicitous in alternative questions (AltQs) like those in (17) and (18).

(17) # mage Ali mehmuni umad ya na?
MAGE Ali party came or no

(18) # mage Ali mehmuni umad ya na-yumad?
MAGE Ali party came or NEG-came

≈ 'Did Ali come to the party or not?'

AltQs, as unbiased questions, express a symmetric interest of the speaker in either of the alternatives offered disjunctively, for example, *Do you come or not?* (Bolinger 1978, Biezma 2009). Therefore, they are not felicitous in settings where either the speaker or the context indicates a bias towards a proposition rather than its alternative.

Roughly speaking, the intended meaning of examples (17) and (18), presented in (19), is the set of answers similar to PQs, as shown in (a). While the question without *mage* is felicitous in neutral contexts (b), we have no subset object as in (c), and the contextual support condition fails. Furthermore, in AltQs, the speaker is open to either of the answers, i.e., she has no idea whether or not Ali came (d). Thus, the speaker's prior expectation of *mage* contradicts the felicitous context for AltQs. In other words, none of the bias conditions of *mage* would be met in contexts that are felicitous for AltQs.

(19) # MAGE did Ali come or not?

a. $[\![$mage did Ali come or not$]\!] = \{come(a), \neg come(a)\}$

b. No contextual evidence is allowed in AltQs.

c. There is no subset object.

d. There is no speaker's prior expectation.

4 Further Issues

It is worth mentioning two outstanding points about *mage*. First, while I have characterized *mage* as anaphoric to the contextual evidence, it can also be used deictically and pick up non-linguistic contextual information as its antecedent. That is, the variable that shrinks the alternative set could be implemented by either being anaphoric to a piece of contextual evidence or deictic to extralinguistic information. The speaker can felicitously use *mage* if she can reasonably assume that the addressee can identify the intended referent. Otherwise, the use of *mage* is infelicitous. For instance, in example (20), the information that they might have an important guest is perceived through extralinguistic evidence, i.e. A and B know that they only clean the house when they have important guests.

(20) **Context:** B begins cleaning the house and asks A for help. Normally, they wouldn't bother cleaning the house unless they were hosting someone important. A was not expecting to have any special guests.

A: mage ki miyâd?
MAGE who comes

'Who does come?'

⤳ The speaker didn't expect any important guests.

Thus, I follow the intentional view, on which reference resolution of the restriction is a pragmatic process that succeeds if the addressee can correctly recognize speaker's referential intention.

Second, the negative expectation in *mage* implicature doesn't need a strong belief/expectation. Regarding the negative raising constructions, the interpretation of negation in the embedded clause, e.g. *Sara expected that Ali doesn't come*, can have a stronger reading in which the speaker is opinionated about the complement proposition. While it feels weaker in the matrix clause, e.g. *Sara didn't expect that Ali comes*, in the sense that the speaker could be unopinionated and the complement clause was not simply in her (active) mental state. In *mage*-Qs, it is possible that either the speaker has some opinion about the restriction or she did not expect the restriction simply because it was not in her mental state.

5 Previous Accounts

Surprisingly, there is little published research on *mage*. Here, I will review Mameni (2010), who introduces *mage* as a genuine interrogative morpheme, similar to *âyâ* 'whether', which only differs in the not-at-issue content. The claim for a genuine interrogative function brings up discussions about *mage* in non-interrogatives and the types of sentences in Farsi.

Let's start with *mage* in non-interrogatives as a conditional operator. *mage* morphologically means 'not if', consisting of *ma-* as an allophone of the negative prefix *na-* and the conditional operator *age* 'if' in Farsi. Hence, it is close enough to translate it as 'unless' in English. Examples (21) and (22) are minimal pairs with the same truth-value meaning: $\neg$Study(*ali*) $\rightarrow$ Fail(*ali*).

(21) age Ali dars na-xune, miofte.
if Ali lesson NEG-read fails

'If Ali doesn't study, he fails.'

(22) Ali miofte, mage dars bexune.
Ali fails unless lesson read

'Ali fails, unless he studies.'

The difference between the examples above is that (22) has an exceptive reading (von Fintel 1992). Roughly interpreting, it indicates '*Except if Ali studies, he doesn't fail*'. In this paper, I focused only on the role of *mage* in interrogatives. Regarding the distinct function and (surface) forms of *mage* in non-interrogatives versus interrogatives, I proposed its second role as a discourse particle.

However, I would not be surprised if we can extend the account to cover both interrogative and non-interrogative conditionals.[1]

Mameni (2010) was aware that the non-interrogative use of *mage* could be an objection against his claim for *mage* as a genuine question morpheme. Although I consider it to be a significant objection, the author briefly addresses it in a footnote by suggesting that if we assume question particles to be morphemes that operate over a proposition and result in multiple possibilities, the objection may not hold (cf. *inquisitive* proposition in Groenendijk and Roelofsen 2009).

Mameni argues that conditionals like (23) (adopted from Mameni 2010:p. 13) proposes two possibilities: the one in which it rains and the one in which it doesn't rain. Thus, truth-conditionally, the sentence denotes both possibilities, including 'Milad comes if it doesn't rain' and 'Milad doesn't come if it rains'.

(23) Milad miad, mage (inke) bârun biâd
Milad comes !Q COM rain comes
'Milad will come only if it doesn't rain.'

He then argues that since *mage* can only scope over irrealis predicates, the speaker does not commit to either of the possibilities. Hence, the conditional meaning is similar to questions, both of which introduce the set of alternatives/partitions.

The discussion about conditionals and and their discourse commitments is beyond the scope of this study. However, in (23), the speaker committs to the consequent *that Milad will come* under the specific circumstance *that it doesn't rain*. That is, if it doesn't rain and Milad doesn't come, he has to retract his commitment. Neither Mameni nor I fully consider the non-interrogative use of *mage* in our studies. However, he underestimates such a role without delving into its properties, and I consider it to be polysemous. While I leave the study of conditionals for future research, I argue that it is a crucial objection for claiming *mage* is *genuinely* a question morpheme.

Let's move on to *mage* in interrogatives. Farsi is an SOV language in which falling ($\downarrow$) and rising ($\uparrow$) intonations are required for declarative and interrogative sentences, respectively. Examples (24) and (25) are minimal pairs, where the former is a declarative (assertion) sentence, and the latter is an interrogative (question).

(24) Ali mehmuni miyâd. $\downarrow$
Ali party comes
'Ali comes to the party.'

(25) Ali mehmuni miyâd? $\uparrow$
Ali party comes
'Does Ali come to the party?'

Mameni claims that in Farsi, the presence of a (polar) question morpheme is optional. He introduces *âyâ* and *mage* as genuine question operators with different implicatures, and he argues that the default reading of non-morpheme questions is the one with *âyâ*. Thus, (25) has the same meaning as (26).[2] I follow his coding for Q and $!Q$ as the question operators for *âyâ* and *mage*, respectively.

(26) âyâ Ali mehmuni miyâd?
Q Ali party comes

(27) mage Ali mehmuni miyâd?
!Q Ali party comes

$\approx$'Does Ali come to the party?'

Mameni proposes that both examples (26) and (27), similar to (25), ask whether or not Ali comes to the party, while they express different not-at-issue contents. *âyâ* in (26) expresses the speaker's ignorance about the answer, while *mage* in (27) signals that the speaker has a (tentative) commitment against the uttered proposition.

Now, let's delve into his argument for proposing *mage* as a genuine question operator. Mameni examines the environments that only select questions and preclude other types of sentences like assertions and commands. He uses the "let me ask you a question" test (Gunlogson 2001) to identify

[1]There are some syntactic and semantic limitations between *age* and *mage*. For instance, **(i)** sentence (21) can maintain the conditional reading by the use of intonation without *age*, while this is not possible for *mage*, **(ii)** the order of the antecedent and consequent clauses generally does not affect *age*-sentences, but it affects the scope of negation in *mage*-sentences, **(iii)** there are constraints on indicative and subjunctive clauses with *mage*. A comprehensive study is required to capture all differences before arguing for any unified analysis of *mage* in both non-interrogatives and interrogatives.

[2]Although Mameni (2010) didn't mention it, (25) and (26) greatly differ in style. That is, *âyâ*-question is very formal and it is often used in written forms, while the rising-question is the canonical form used in usual/colloquial settings. As a Farsi speaker, I hardly remember if I have ever used *âyâ*, even in formal contexts. Furthermore, following his claim for the default reading of (rising) non-morpheme questions with *âyâ*-operator, the ignorant implicature of *âyâ* in (26) is expressed in (25) as well, which I am not sure about. The discussion about the difference between rising polar questions and *âyâ* questions is beyond the scope of this paper.

the questions from other types. Example (28) is adopted from Mameni (2010): p. 14.

(28) azat ye soâl beporsam, ...
from one question ask
Let me ask you a question,...

a. âyâ Milâd raft?
Q Milad left
≈'Did Milad leave?'

b. mage Milâd raft?
!Q Milad left
≈'Did Milad leave?'

c. # Milâd raft.
Milad left
'Milad left.'

d. # boro!
leave
'Leave!'

Regarding the unacceptability of the declarative in (c) and the imperative in (d) compared to (a) and (b), Mameni concludes that *âyâ* and *mage* are genuine interrogative morphemes. He did not provide further explanation or argument for this (crucial) claim. He only challenges the critics, stating that if *mage* is not a question morpheme, it is almost impossible to explain why declarative sentences with *mage* are necessarily interpreted as questions. Notice that Mameni provides sentences with *mage* in falling intonation and claims that such sentences have a question reading. Overall, the argument presented by the author for *mage* as a question morpheme is based on its presence in interrogatives, and in order to support this argument, he stipulates conditional sentences as inquisitive.

I start with his examples of questions with falling intonation. In Farsi, rising intonation is necessary for polar questions, regardless of the presence of a question marker such as *âyâ* or *mage*. None of his examples with falling intonation on *mage*-questions were considered felicitous by my native speaker informants, including the author (some informants interpreted them as conditionals, with an elided antecedent).

Furthermore, while multiple Wh-words can form a single WhQ as in (29), using a double polar question marker shouldn't be felicitous, as claimed by Mameni in examples (30)-(31) (adopted from Mameni 2010: p. 12).

(29) ki či xarid?
who what bought
'Who bought what?'

(30) ??âyâ mage Milad raft?
Q !Q Milad left

(31) *mage âyâ Milad raft?
!Q Q Milad left

Mameni footnoted that the judgments were inaccurate since many speakers reject (31), but find (30) possible. The author suggests two hatches for the judgment variation.[3] He, however, rejects these hatches as they could not explain why the acceptability of (30) is degraded, in addition to why the movement of *mage* is restricted when it is preceded by *âyâ*. Therefore, he considers the sentences unacceptable and claims that the two morphemes cannot co-occur.

I share the intuition with the informants in which (30) sounds better than (31). What is irritating and degrades the acceptability of the combination of *âyâ* and *mage* is more about their style difference. That is, while *âyâ* is used in very formal and literary settings, *mage* is a colloquial particle. A native speaker might find the examples better in a context where the speaker should be polite and formal, but also wants to be friendly and informal. In such cases, it is widely common for the speaker to use elements from different styles to express both formal politeness (e.g., *âyâ*) and informal friendliness (e.g., *mage*). It seems weird but is practically common.

For instance, speaking with grandparents, on one hand, the grandchild wants to be polite regarding the age difference. On the other hand, she has a friendly relationship with her grandparents that allows her to speak in a friendly/informal style. In such cases, as in (32), the grandchild sometimes uses the pronoun *šomâ* plural PL-you (instead of *to* singular SG-you), but she conjugates the verb in singular. Syntactically, the structure is ungrammatical, but pragmatically it is commonly used.

(32) šomâ mehmuni miya-i?
you-PL party comes-SG
'Do you come to the party?'

In the context of (33), we can also see that the mother uses *šomâ* PL-you to treat her kid po-

[3](i) He said that regarding the fact that *mage* is free to occur sentence-medially and sentence-finally, he assumes that if *mage* precedes *âyâ*, it cannot move. Thus, (31) is ungrammatical according to the informants compared to the better form in (30). (ii) It could be the case that since the meaning of *âyâ* questions is distinct from the meaning of *mage*, in marginal cases like (30), the question is interpreted as *mage*-meaning. This is possible by hypothesising that there is a covert *âyâ* morpheme in every *mage* question.

litely, while she conjugates the verbs in singular, as they have an informal/friendly mother-child relationship. Now, using formal *âyâ* and informal *mage* sounds reasonable. While the order (*âyâ mage*) and (*mage âyâ*) don't matter here, the former is generally preferred because the default position of *âyâ* is sentence-initial.

(33) **Context:** In child psychology, it is suggested to speak politely with children to show that the parents respect their character. A is a young mother following this comment. She and her kid are at a party. She told the kid that he is allowed to have two cookies. She sees that the kid starts eating the fourth cookie...

A: âyâ mage man be šomâ na-goftam
Q MAGE I to you-PL NEG-tell
faqat dota širini mitun-i boxor-i?
only two cookie can-SG eat-SG
'Didn't I tell you that you can only have two cookies?'

If *mage* is genuinely a question morpheme, its co-occurrence with *âyâ* shouldn't be possible, specifically because they express implicatures that conflict with each other. Finally, while polar question operators like *âyâ* cannot occur with other Wh-words as in (34), *mage* can be easily used in WhQs as in (35).

(34) # âyâ ki miad?
Q who comes

(35) mage ki miad?
MAGE who comes
'MAGE who does come?'

Note that Mameni did not work on WhQs, and he left it for future studies to extend his account to WhQs. I am not sure what exactly a question might ask, carrying both polar and constituent question operators. Thus, taking *mage* as a question morpheme could not explain the data in (35).

6 Conclusion

In this paper, I investigated the discursive function of particle *mage* in interrogatives. While the literature reported that *mage* in polar questions, [*mage* ϕ?], implicates speaker's prior belief against the uttered proposition ϕ, I presented that the felicitous context for the particle requires contextual evidence towards ϕ. I then extended the analysis to *mage* in WhQs, where the required contextual evidence restricts the alternative set of answers. Therefore, I proposed the meaning and felicity condition of particle *mage* based on the *answerhood* notation in interrogatives.

The proposal for the role of two types of biases, including speaker's bias and contextual bias, in *mage*-questions could explain the data in both polar and constituent questions. Furthermore, it provides a natural explanation for the unacceptability of *mage* in alternative questions, as AltQs cannot be used in biased contexts. While the literal meaning of *mage* in conditionals is far-fetched from its bias-sensitive function in interrogatives, I leave the discussion about *mage* in non-interrogatives for future studies.

References

Biezma, M. (2009). *Alternative vs Polar Questions: the cornering effect*, Volume 19.

Bolinger, D. (1978). Yes/no questions are not alternative questions. In *H. Hiz, Questions*, pp. 87–105. Reidel Publishing Company, Dordrecht, Holland.

Büring, D. and C. Gunlogson (2000, 01). Aren't positive and negative polar questions the same?

Domaneschi, F., M. Romero, and B. Braun (2017). Bias in polar questions: Evidence from English and German production experiments. *Glossa: a journal of general linguistics 21*.

Groenendijk, J. and F. Roelofsen (2009, 01). Inquisitive semantics and pragmatics.

Gunlogson, C. (2001). Phd dissertation, University of California Santa Cruz.

Hamblin, C. L. (1973). Questions in montague English. *Foundations of Language 10*(1), 41–53.

Karttunen, L. (1977). Syntax and semantic of questions. *Linguistics Philosophy 1*, 3–44.

Ladd, D. (1981). A first look at the semantics and pragmatics of negative questions and tag questions.

Lindner, K. (1991). Wir sind ja doch alte bekannte. *The Use of Germanjaanddochas Modal Particles. In W. Abraham (ed.)Discourse Particles. Amsterdam/Philadelphia:John Benjamins Publishing Company.*, 163–201.

Mameni, M. (2010). *Epistemic Implicatures and Inquisitive Bias: a Multidimensional Semantics for Polar Questions*. Ma dissertation, Simon Fraser University.

Martinez, M. L. M. (2003). *Contextual Variables*. Phd dissertation, University of Connecticut.

Roelofsen, F. and D. F. Farkas (2015). Polarity particle responses as a window onto the interpretation of questions and assertions. *Language 91*(2), 359–414.

Romero, M. and C. Han (2004). On negative yes/no questions. *Linguistics and Philosophy 27*, 609–658.

Theiler, N. (2021). *Denn* as a highlighting-sensitive particle. *Linguistics and Philosophy 44*.

von Fintel, K. (1992). Exceptive conditionals: The meaning of unless. In *Proceedings of North East Linguistics Society*, Volume 22.

Zimmermann, M. (2011). Discourse particles. pp. 2012–2038.

Dynamic Questions: Evidence from Mandarin Think–"Xiang"

Anshun Zheng
School of Philosophy Psychology and Language sciences
University of Edinburgh
A.Zheng-3@sms.ed.ac.uk

Abstract

This paper investigates the clausal embedding pattern of the Mandarin verb "xiang" (think) and reveals its internal anti-interrogative nature, with the possibility of "xiang Q" in certain cases. Through various stativity tests, I establish that the results are consistent with the generalization proposed by Özyıldız (2021), with "minor" deviations observed in the stativity of "xiang P" and the correlation with neg-raising. Additionally, I employ a semantic shift perspective to explain instances of neg-raising failure. Overall, this study sheds light on the unique characteristics of the verb "xiang" and contributes to a better cross-linguistic understanding of CP selection.

1 Introduction

Predicates are able to embed different types of clausal complements. For example, "think" usually selects the declarative clauses while "wonder" takes interrogative ones only. Traditionally, this selection was attributed to syntactic factors, but since Grimshaw (1979), it has been viewed as more of a semantic choice. A series of works have been devoted to revealing the role of semantic factors in complement selection including factivity and veridicality hypotheses (Hintikka, 1975; Egré, 2008), reductive approach (Q-to-P reduction: Karttunen 1977; Lahiri et al. 2002; Spector and Egré 2015, P-to-Q reduction: Uegaki 2015), uniform approach (inquisitive semantics: Theiler et al. 2018, 2019, a systematic review see Uegaki 2019) and the stativity hypothesis (Özyıldız, 2021). Given most of the studies attended to English exclusively, the present investigation into Mandarin aims to provide more cross-linguistic evidence to the issue. In Mandarin, predicates taking CP can be classified as responsives (±Wh), anti-rogatives (-Wh), and rogatives (+Wh) as in English. Canonical examples are given below.

(1) Ask, Rogative (+Wh)

Wo wen ni mali zai na
I ask you Mary exist where

'I ask you where Mary is.'

(2) Know, Responsive (±Wh)

a. Wo zhidao mali zai na
I know Mary exist where
'I know where Mary is.'

b. Wo zhidao mali zai jia
I know Mary exist home
'I know Mary is at home.'

(3) Think, Anti-rogative (-Wh)

Wo renwei mali chi-le fan
I think Mary eat-perf rice

'I think Mary has eaten.'

Among these predicates, "think" is particularly intricate in many ways. The English word "think" can have several counterparts in Mandarin including "renwei", "juede", "ganjue", "yiwei", "xiang" and "sikao"[1]. Despite a little nuance, all of them can be used to report thoughts. However, they differ in terms of their CP selection pattern. For example, "renwei" and "xiang" are canonically anti-rogative in bare form (4a,4b), while "sikao" is rogative (4c) [2].

(4) "xiang", "renwei" cf. "sikao"

a. *Wo xiang zenme zuo ti
I think how do question

[1] Glass (2020) gave translations to some of these terms: renwei(neutral think), xiang(believe/want), juede(feel that), and she also discussed the false belief think, "yiwei". "Ganjue" is similar to "juede" with the nuance of "sensual". "Sikao" is a more formal way to say think, closer to "ponder".

[2] This bare form "sikao" plus Q in (4c) sounds not good to some informants, and an aspect marker like "zai(-prog)" will make it work better. Since it is acceptable to some informants, I suggest it may be regional. However, there is a consensus that "xiang" is less natural with an embedded Q than "sikao".

Proceedings of the 4th Workshop on Inquisitiveness Below and Beyond the Sentence Boundary (InqBnB4), pages 40–49
June 20, 2023.

b. *Wo renwei zenme zuo ti
I think how do questions

c. Wo sikao zenme zuo ti
I think how do questions
'I'm thinking how to solve questions.'

To make matters worse, the selection pattern is not fixed (cf. 4a, 5), as was observed in Özyıldız (2021)'s analysis of "think Q".

(5) Wo zai xiang zenme zuo ti
I -prog think how do questions
'I'm thinking how to solve questions.'

The instability in Özyıldız's account is due to stativity. I will call it the stativity hypothesis. He showed that embedding types are correlated to stativity of the event structure, so the selection is not purely lexical but is highly dependent on the environment (Table 1, see also Roberts 2019). For instance, he claimed the availability of "think Q" is from a dynamic environment[3]. His account works smoothly with English "think", but will it be safe and sound in Mandarin as well? For many reasons, this paper selects "xiang" as its primary object of study. Unlike some other equivalents (e.g., "renwei"), "xiang" shows an aspectual alternation, which is crucial, since we will use the compatibility with certain aspects to test for stativity. Additionally, "xiang" does not appear to allow for a neg-raising reading, which deviates from the correlation suggested in Özyıldız's account. Finally, "xiang" shows a very complex lexical semantics, which may reveal more intricacies and interactions for future research to consider

	Embedded Q	Neg-raising(with P)
Stative	-	+
Dynamic	+	-

Table 1: Özyıldız's idea of correlation between stativity, question embedding and neg-rasing

There are mainly two goals of this paper. Firstly, it seeks to provide empirical evidence and tests to examine the embedded question compatibility of "xiang". Secondly, it aims to probe how much the stativity hypothesis accommodates this Mandarin equivalent of *think*.

The structure is organised as follows. §2 provides a brief overview of the various meaning entries of "xiang" in Mandarin and explains how its meaning might be determined. §3 presents an analysis of the lexical selectional pattern of "xiang" [4], while §4 and §5 examine how the stativity hypothesis can be applied to explain the occurrences of "xiang Q" and how neg-raising is problematic in the case of "xiang".

2 Lexical semantics and pragmatics of "xiang"

"Xiang" can have several interpretations in different linguistic contexts. There are roughly four interpretations: (1) think and assume (2) hope and want (3) pine for, and (4) recall and remember[5]. Sometimes, the boundary between these entries are not clear-cut. (6) shows the same phrasing can lead to different readings under different contexts, namely asking for opinions and imperatives[6].

(6) Ni xiang zenme zuo
you think how do
'how do you **want** to do.'
'you **think** how to do.'

The interpretation of "xiang" is highly dependent on the its environment. Some potential factors that can trigger the semantic shift include: (1) modals and aspect markers in the embedded clause[7] (2) the presence of negation (see §5), and (3) status as an imperative (6). However, the details of these triggers are beyond the scope of this paper[8]. In the following sections, I endeavor to control for these

[3]However, Özyıldız also admitted it remains unclear where the dynamicity comes from. The reason he thinks a structure is dynamic is because it passes several dynamicity tests.

[4]By bare form, I mean there are no extra aspect markers or collocations so it is not in a sense of inflection.

[5]A summary of usages of "xiang" mentioned in (Lü, 1999).

[6]In (6), "xiang" combines with a phrase that contains the wh-word "zenme" (how), which seems to contradict with my claim that it is anti-rogative. I will explain it in §3, where I will present evidence of the question not being an embedded Q.

[7]

(7) a. Wo xiang ta chifan
I think he eat
'I **want** him to eat.'

b. Wo xiang ta chi-le-fan
I think he eat-perf
'I **think** he has eaten.'

(7a) and (7b) manifest the aspect marker being a trigger.

[8]Presenting these factors is to make readers aware that there are more interactions happening than what is described in the paper. For readers who are interested, check Xiao and McEnery (2004) and He (1992) on Mandarin aspects and Biq (1991) on second person pronoun influence to get a flavor of the details. However, in terms of selection, it is still understudied.

factors and focus on situations where "xiang" is used to mean "think"[9].

3 Plain "Xiang" does not take Q

"Xiang" alone shows significant incompatibility with question embeddings (4a). The following examples further confirm this.

(8) a. *Wo/ta xiang ta shi shei
I/He think he is who
'I/He am/is thinking who he is.'

b. *Wo/ta xiang ta hui chi shenme
I/He think he will eat what
#'I/He think(s) what he will eat.'

You may be wondering why I did not provide examples in the second person. That is because "xiang" seems to be compatible with questions when used with second person subjects (6, 9). Does it mean "xiang" is not anti-rogative but responsive? Probably not. I posit that in these second person cases, the question is not an embedded clause, but rather a root question, which is possible because Mandarin is a wh-in-situ language. Therefore, we need to first differentiate between embedded questions and root questions[10].

(9) Ni xiang ta hui chi shenme
you think he will eat what
'what do you think he will eat?'

3.1 -Ne test as a test for matrix Q

"-Ne" is a particle that is compatible with wh-questions and shares the scope with the wh-phrase in Mandarin (10a, 10b). Canonical wh-questions usually do not need "-ne" and it turns out "-ne" can serve as a matrix clause scope marker to distinguish root questions from embedded questions. Apart from the question reading, "-ne" can also lead to "emphatic" reading and "imperfective" reading.

(10) a. Ta zai na (ne)
He exist where (-ne)
'where is him?'

b. Ta zai gan shenme (ne)
He -prog do what (-ne)
'what is he doing?'

Dong (2018) pointed out that this particle is not able to take a scope of embedded questions. Rogative predicates like "wen"(ask) usually force an embedded question reading. Hence, they do not co-occur with "-ne", which is incompatible with the embedding scope. For example, (11) is ungrammatical if it intends to give an embedded question reading, while it still can have an emphatic interpretation–"Zhangsan even asked the question!"[11], or an imperfective reading–"Zhangsan is asking me the question, don't bother me".

(11) Ask (Dong, 2018, 29)

*Zhangsan wen wo shei mai-le shu ne
Zhangsan ask me who buy-perf books -ne

'Zhangsan asked me who bought books.'

According to Dong's account, anti-rogatives are limited to having only matrix clause scope, making them compatible with the "wh-ne" structure (12).

(12) Believe (Dong, 2018, 30)

Zhangsan xiangxin shei mai-le shu ne
Zhangsan believe who buy-perf books -ne

'who does Zhangsan believe bought books?'

However, in the case of responsives, which can have both matrix and embedding scope, Dong claimed that as long as the matrix clause scope is available, the structure remains well-formed[12].

In summary, "wh-ne" construction can be utilised to test for whether an in-situ question is embedded or not. As (13) shows, the second person "xiang + Q" passes the test, leading to a root question reading, indicating (13) at least has a reading as a matrix question, even though it looks on the surface like it embeds a question.

[9]One intriguing question that remained to be considered is why conceptually similar words associated with psychoactivity encompass vastly different meanings. While this paper does not thoroughly address the question, one approach is to examine it through prototype theory. For instance, words like "recall" and "miss" can be seen as prototypical of "xiang", but not of "think". Some accounts, such as Xu et al. (2013), view this issue as a distinction between cognition, emotion, and motivation (another decompositional approach see also Bondarenko (2020)). According to Xu et al.'s account, the difference between "xiang" and "think" can be attributed to a division difference between these elements.

[10]Note that (8a) and (8b) are not considered well-formed, no matter the question is embedded or not. The purpose of contrasting them with (9) is to demonstrate that in second person cases, a question interpretation is feasible. The subsequent discussion in section 3.1 aims to unravel whether "xiang" can inherently take a question complement with a person that allows for a question interpretation.

[11]The reading is possible under contexts where the speaker is surprised or acts mean to the subject.

[12]There is a minor point to mention regarding Dong's account of responsives. It is possible that his examples of responsives being ungrammatical could be due to factive islands. However, this matter is not directly pertinent to the main focus of this paper, so I won't delve into it extensively.

(13) 2nd person + "xiang"

Ni xiang ta hui chi shenme ne
you think he will eat what -ne

'what do you think he will eat?'

It is important to highlight that the root question reading with "xiang" plus "wh-ne" is not valid in other persons (e.g., *adding "-ne" to 8a,8b), implying there possibly exists a person effect that does not exist in English, but unfortunately, this paper will not address what this effect could be[13]. A detailed "-ne" test result is shown as in Table 2. Apart from the findings on question readings, I noticed the emphatic reading is more compatible with predicates that allow for [+Wh]. This implies that Mandarin wh-phrases may also be tinted with [+Excl] even if it is not used in an exclamtive construction like English.

Predicates	*Root Question*	*Emphatic*	*Imperfective*
$Renwei(think, -Wh)$	+	−	#
$Xiang(think, -Wh)$	+	#	+
$Sikao(think, +Wh)$	−	+	+
$Zhidao(know, \pm Wh)$	#	+	−
$Wen(ask, +Wh)$	−	+	+

Table 2: The available interpretations of predicates of different selectional types in "wh-ne" environment. Several trends revealed here are: (1) anti-rogatives can have root question reading[a] (2) only predicates allowing (+WH) can be emphatic.

[a]Responsives (e.g., tell) "can" have root question reading as well but most of them are under restrictions of factive islands.

3.2 Evidence from question-response pairs

The "-ne" test identifies that what are in the idiosyncratic second person cases are matrix questions, rescuing my claim that "xiang" does not take question complements. Here in this section, I intend to provide further evidence to show that the embedded scope is actually not available.

Matrix questions and matrix statements with question-complements differ in their ability to elicit responses. The former is designed to seek new information, while the latter has the capability to prompt a simple yes/no response. For instance, a sentence like "What do you think he will eat?" can elicit a response like "(I think he will eat) cake." (cf. (12)), whereas a sentence like "She knows what he will do." can elicit a response like "No, she doesn't." (cf. (11)).

According to (14), even without a particle that specifically triggers a matrix scope interpretation, the reading of the sentence still remains as a matrix question. This implies that the availability of an embedded scope is not possible, thereby supporting my argument that the bare form "xiang" does not accept wh-complements.

(14) Ni xiang ta hui chi shenme
you think he will eat what
'what do you think he will eat?'

a. *'dui, wo xiang.' (Yes, I am.)

b. 'wo xiang ta hui chi yu.'(I think he will eat fish.)

4 Influences from the environment: stative or dynamic

However, there exist certain scenarios in which the verb "xiang" can take embedded questions as its complement. These situations include imperatives, verbs that imply force, and certain aspect markers[14], which roughly mirrors what Özyıldız (2021) observed in English "think+Q".

(15) Imperatives

Ni xiang zhe ti zenme zuo (*-ne), wo
you think this question how do (*-ne), I
xiang xia yi ti
think next one question

'You think how to solve this question, I'll think about the next one.'

(16) Force

Wo ba rang wo xiang zenme zhuan
my father make me think how earn
qian (*-ne)
money (*-ne)

'My father makes me think how to make money.'

(17) Some aspect markers

Wo zai-/xiang/-le/-guo xia yi bu qi
I think-prog/-perf/-exp next one step chess
zenme zou (*-ne)
how walk (*-ne)

[13]This is in contrast to English matrix clause questions with "think", which can be formed in all persons given the appropriate context (e.g., what does he think we should do?).

[14]Some informants, including the author, found "sikao" (the possibly rogative "think") is more natural with verbs of force type. When "xiang" is under force, it just means "sikao". "Xiang" with durative marker, most informants felt, is more acceptable with declaratives such as "wo xiang-zhe ni mingtian youkong, women keyi yiqi qu guangjie" (I think-dur you are available, so we can go shopping together.).

'I am/have thinking/thought what is the next move.'

According to Özyıldız's analysis, this alternation is determined by the event structure, the environment in which the verb is used. The alternation occurred at the lexical level (e.g., within the vP) by taking different arguments (Q or P), but the effect is observed at a higher level (e.g., the AspP). This observation also applies in Mandarin. For example, the verb "wang" (forget) requires an obligatory perfective marker "le" when used alone (Figure 1), but the marker becomes optional when there is a VP complement (Figure 2). Thus, the aspectual nature of the vP could be determined by analyzing higher-level structures.

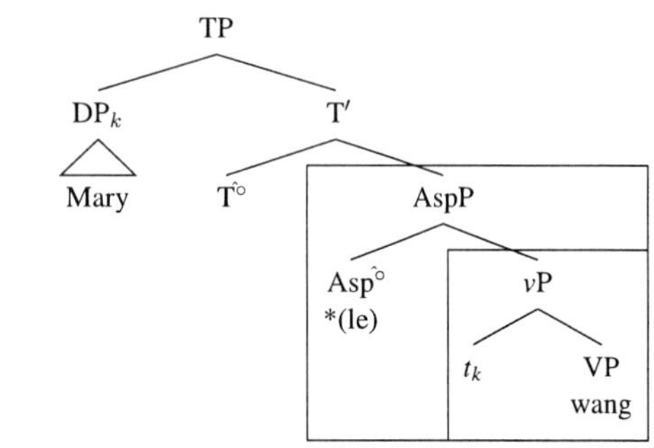

Figure 1: "Mary forgot."

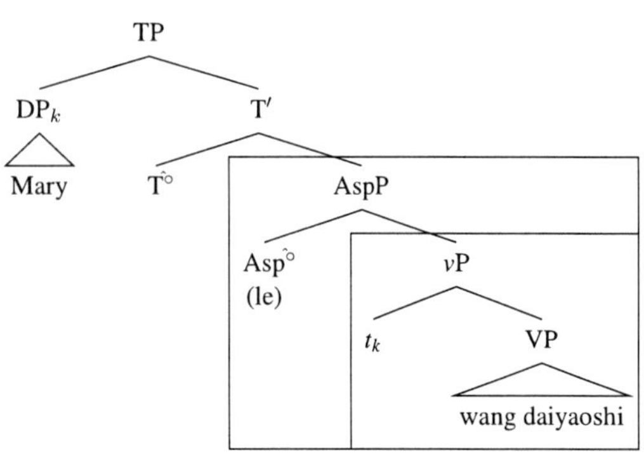

Figure 2: "Mary forgot to take the key."

In Özyıldız (2021), several tests were employed to examine the stativity of the vP (e.g., present simple and progressive interpretations, and narrative progression) to show that the resulting event description of "think Q" is dynamic while that of "think P" is either stative or dynamic. In the upcoming section, we will explore whether this generalisation holds in the case of "xiang".

Generalisation (Özyıldız, 2021, 43)

a. when 'think' composes with a question, the resulting description must be dynamic.

b. when 'think' composes with a declarative, the resulting description may be stative or it may be dynamic.

4.1 Stativity tests

-Zhe test "-Zhe" is a durative aspect marker in Mandarin. It usually combines with a dynamic verb such as "xiao"(smile) and "zou"(walk). However, the resulting situation is stative. For example, (18a-18b) describe how a person eats and enters the room, namely, the manner. Thus, there is no clear temporal contour of the events without a clear reference to the initial or the ending point.

(18) a. Ta xiao-zhe chi fan
He/she smile-dur eat rice
'He/she is eating with a smile/while smiling'

b. Ta zou-zhe jinru-le yige fangjian
He/she walk-dur enter-perf one room
'He/she entered into a room by walking'

According to He (1992), "-zhe" denotes an exclusive stative situation. He observed that "-zhe" co-occurs with some stative predicates or with action verbs to express manner or background so that the situation as a whole is stative regardless of the innate temporality of the verb itself [15]. Even if "-zhe" is not helpful in distinguishing the stativity of the lexical aspect, it hints the stativity of the situation as a whole, which is sufficient for our purpose.

(19) "Xiang-zhe + Q/P"

a. *Wo xiang-zhe xia yi bu qi zenme zou
I think-dur next one step chess how walk
'I am thinking what is the next move.'

b. Wo xiang-zhe women mingtian keyi qu guangjie
I think-dur we tomorrow can go shopping
'I think we can go shopping tomorrow.'

[15] Xiao and McEnery (2004) has a slightly different take on "-zhe". They mentioned the same phrase "chuan-zhe" (put on/wear-zhe) can describe both dynamic and stative situation: "he is wearing the body armour all day long" (stative) and "he rushed towards the room while he was still putting on his overcoat" (dynamic). They claimed the stative situation is an extension of dynamic event. But the resulting event description is stative after all.

According to (19a), it is evident that the structure "xiang Q" cannot coexist with "-zhe", which results in a constrained stative context. This suggests that "xiang Q" may require a dynamic environment and possess the trait of non-stative. Conversely, the structure "xiang P" (see 19b) exhibits a strong compatibility with "-zhe", indicating that it can be internally stative. These findings align with the generalization in terms of stativity.

4.2 Dynamicity

In addition to looking at stativity, there are also a variety of diagnostics to test whether a sentence is dynamic, for instance, progressive, pseudo-cleft and agentive adverbials (Dowty, 1979; Olsen, 1994; Özyıldız, 2021). All of these three tests will be utilised.

Progessive -Zai In English, dynamic predicates are usually able to combine with progressives to express an on-going event (e.g., be running) and do not usually coexist with typical stative predicates (e.g., *be liking). In Mandarin, the progressive marker "-zai" also usually occurs in dynamic situations. Xiao and McEnery (2004) conducted a corpus study and found that out of 88 instances (not necessarily "zai-xiang") with "-zai", 86 of them are describing a dynamic situation[16]. From examples (17, 20a), we can roughly confirm that "xiang Q" is compatible with progressive aspect, indicating it may require a dynamic environment. On the contrary, "xiang P" resists suffixing "-zai" (20b), implying that "xiang P" may not be dynamic, which differs from English, where "think P" can be dynamic.

(20) "Zai-xiang + Q/P"

a. Wo zai-xiang ruhe zuo fan
I think-prog how make rice
'I am thinking how to cook.'

b. *Wo zai-xiang ta chi-guo fan-le
I think-prog he eat-exp rice-LE
'I am thinking he has eaten.'

Pseudo-clefting According to Dowty (1979), structures such as "what he did was..." can only be used with non-stative verbs. For instance, "what he did was run" is grammatical, whereas "what he did was like" is not. This same pattern may also exist in Mandarin, as demonstrated in examples (21a,21b). The literal translation of the original construction in (21a,21b) is "the thing that he/she did was", which differs from the English pseudo-cleft. This difference could be due to the fact that free relatives and wh-phrases are distinct in Mandarin. However, despite the structural differences, these constructions should have a similar function.

(21) What he did was...

a. Ta zuo-le de shiqing shi
He/she do-perf -relative thing is
paobu
run
'What he/she did was run.'

b. *Ta zuo-le de shiqing shi
He/she do-perf -relative thing is
xihuan mao
like cat
'what he/she did was like cats.'

Example (22a) is acceptable under a context like checking against a to-do list, while example (22b) is unacceptable under any circumstances. The results, again, show "xiang Q" is dynamic and "xiang P" is not.

(22) Clefting + "xiang + Q/P"

a. Ta zuo-le de shiqing shi
He/she do-perf -relative thing is
xiang wanfan chi shenme
think dinner eat what
'what he/she did was think what to eat for dinner.'

b. *Ta zuo-le de shiqing shi
He/she do-perf -relative thing is
xiang mali chi-le wanfan
think Mary eat-perf dinner
'what he/she did was think Mary has had dinner.'

Agentivity tests Agentivity is another feature that is considered closely related to dynamicity. Diagnostics includes "force/persuade" type verbs, imperatives, agent-oriented adverbs (Lakoff, 1966; Dowty, 1979). We have seen the compatibility of the first two in (15,16)[17]. Here, we will test against agentive adverbials. The equivalents of the agentive adverbials used in English are "jiaojide(worriedly)", "zixide"(carefully), and "guyide"(deliberately) in Mandarin.

(23) Worriedly, carefully, intentionally + "xiang + Q/P"

[16]The rest two are stage-level stative words such as "hungry", and "happy", in contrast with individual-level stative words like "clever".

[17]I should also note here "xiang P" shows ungrammaticality in these two situations.

a. Wo jiaojide/zixide/?*guyide
I worriedly/carefully/intentionally
xiang ta zai na
think he exist where

'I am worriedly/carefully/intentionally thinking where he is.'

b. Wo *worriedly/*zixide/*guyide
I worriedly/carefully/intentionally
xiang ta chi-le fan
think he eat-perf rice

'I worriedly/carefully/intentionally think he has eaten.'

Examples (23a) and (23b) demonstrate that "xiang Q" can be used with some selected adverbials, while "xiang P" cannot be used with the same adverbials. This suggests that "xiang Q" involves some degree of agency, while "xiang P" does not. This conclusion is in line with the results of the other two tests, which indicate that "xiang Q" is dynamic while "xiang P" is stative. However, this agentive adverbial test is not reliable in a few ways: (1) The acceptability of the result sentences depends on how natural the collocation is rather than the stativity. (2) They can appear with some stative words (i.e., asleep). But, essentially, all three tests lead to the same conclusion about the nature of "xiang Q" and "xiang P".

4.3 Eventive contexts

Narrative progression Before coming to the end, I would like to discuss the deviation from English "think P" that "xiang P" is not dynamic under tests in §4. In fact, there is a possibility where "xiang P" is dynamic. Under the theory of temporal discourse representation (Dowty 1986; Abusch 2014 and references therein)[18], a sequence of situations can be constructed as : Given a sequence of sentences $S_1...S_n$ with respective described situations as $\sigma_1...\sigma_n$, if a sentence S_i is stative, then temporally σ_i and σ_{i-1} is overlapping ($\sigma_i \circ_t \sigma_{i-1}$), otherwise, for any sentence S_t, its situation σ_t should show progression ($\sigma_{t-1} \leq_t \sigma_t$). That is, if "xiang P" by any chance is dynamic, the utterance containing "xiang P" should successfully show narrative progression, without showing overlapping or an oddity from overlapping[19].

(25) Zhangsan zoujin-le shitang. Ta xiang ta
Zhangsan enter-perf restaurant. He think he
yingai hui chi yu. Ta dian-le yi
probably will eat fish. He order-perf one
fen yu.
-CLS fish

'Zhangsan entered a restaurant. He thought he probably would eat fish. He ordered fish.'

(25) shows a valid progression in narration time without oddity[20], indicating "xiang P" is possibly eventive. However, I also found out that the progression also works for "know"(zhidao), a canonically stative verb. This opens several possibilities, if the test is effective in Mandarin: (1)"Xiang P" is dynamic. (2) The canonical stative "zhidao(know)" is also potentially dynamic like "xiang". (3) The incompatibility between progressive marker and potential dynamic "xiang P" suggests "-zai" may be special.

¬ think P One argument put forth by Özyıldız (2021) in favor of the dynamic "think P" is based on the observation that the negation of this expression can be used to describe an activity in which the attitude holder is not involved at the topic time. Through examples provided in Özyıldız (2021, 43), it is shown how "think P" can resist being interpreted as a background belief when negated, thereby implying an eventive interpretation.

(26) a. When Esra knocked, I was thinking that she was in Mexico. [Background belief]

b. When Ersa knocked, I wasn't think that she was in Mexico. [As activity]

However, in our analysis (see also §5), we do not observe such a change due to negation because

[18]Özyıldız (2021) also used a similar narrative progression test, which works by identifying whether an inserted simple past event advances the narrative time. Since Mandarin does not have "simple past", I reckon this test requires a bit more work.

[19]The resulting oddity was pointed out by and Lascarides and Asher (1993) and further explained by Abusch (2014). If a succession is inferred in an eventive situation followed by stative situation, there will be an oddity (24).

(24) An example adapted from Lascarides and Asher (1993)

#Zhangsan yin-le bisai. Ta zai jia.
Zhangsan win-perf competition. He at home.

'Zhangsan won the race. He was at home.'

[20]This test is not straightforward, as we can see a sentence like "when he entered the restaurant, he already knew/thought that he should order fish, then he ordered fish" can pass the progression test as well.

obtaining expressions like "¬ xiang (think) P" or "¬ xiang (think)-prog P" is nearly impossible.

In summary, "xiang Q" and "xiang P" alternates with a change in stativity in Mandarin, which supports the central view of Özyıldız (2021), with a difference that "xiang P" may not be dynamic. Because the diagnostics for stativity might be language-dependent, and the diagnostics for Mandarin is still understudied. More research is needed before arriving at a definitive conclusion.

5 Neg-raising?

Another observation of the stativity hypothesis, if not the core claim, is neg-raising property (Table 1). This connection between stativity and neg-raising was suggested by Özyıldız (2021); Jeretic and Özyıldız (2022). In addition, Theiler et al. (2019) pointed out a link between anti-rogativity and neg-rasing, which also suggested "xiang" as a potential anti-rogative predicate should allow for neg-raising. However, a thorny issue that must be addressed before establishing the connection is how neg-raising works in Mandarin.

Negation in Mandrain There are several ways to do negations in Mandarin including "bu" negation, "mei" negation, and "bie" negation[21]. Roughly, "bu" is more like English not, a pure negation, "mei" is tinted with imperfective meaning, and "bie" is an imperative negation (27).

(27) Bu/Mei/Bie zuo
-Neg do
Bu: '(I) don't do (that).'
Mei: '(I) haven't done/didn't do (that).'
Bie: '(you) don't do (that)!'

Neg-raising usually works with "bu" negator as shown below (28)[22].

(28) Bu Neg-raising
Wo bu xiang ta lai
I -NEG want he come
'I don't want him to come.'
→ I want him not to come.

If we use different negators to negate "xiang(think) P" in (29), the results are shown in examples (30a,30b). If neg-raising were possible, negating (29) would result in an inference such as "I think he is not sick". However, neither (30a) nor (30b) produces this inference even in the ideal stative and declarative setting, rather, we get a bouletic interpretation of "xiang".

(29) Wo xiang ta shengbing-le
I think he sick-LE
'I **think** he is sick.'

(30) a. "Bu" negation
Wo bu-xiang ta shengbing
I Neg-think he sick
'I don't **want** him to be sick.'

b. "Mei" negation
Wo mei-xiang ta shengbing
I Neg-think he sick
'(you think I wish he is sick, but) I don't **want** him to be sick.'

I assume this is because a meaning shift happened due to negation, from "think" to "want" (29-30b) or the opposite (31a,31b)[23]. These examples show that "xiang" meaning "think" prefers a positive environment but can tolerate a negative one if the meaning of "want" is not available such as in an imperative sentence.

(31) a. Ni xiang ta lai bangmang
You think he come help
'You **want** him to help (you).'

b. "Bie" negation
Ni bie-xiang ta hui lai bangmang
You Neg-think he will come help
'Don't **think** that he will help (you).'

The only possible scenario for testing neg-raising with "xiang"(think) is in an environment as in (31b) since "bie" does not cause meaning shift to "want". Unfortunately, "Bie" seems not to allow for neg-raising inference. Take "juede"(think) as an example since it is a valid neg-raising verb under "bu"

[21] Ernst (1995) and Xiao and McEnery (2008) investigated how "bu" and "mei" differ and their interaction. Biq (1989) explored more about pragmatics or paralinguistic usages of negation.

[22] According to Xiang (2013), the neg-raising is asymmetrical between "bu" and "mei" as she observed that "xiang"(want) gets a neg-raising inference in "bu" but not in "mei".

[23] Examples (31a,31b) are there to show the possibility of the semantic shift in the opposite way. But the meaning change is not always happening. For example, "ni xiang taiduo le" (you think too much) → "ni bie xiang taiduo le" (don't think too much). Hence, the pattern is: "want" shifts to "think" under imperative negation, while the opposite under the other two types.

negation[24]. As (32) shows, the neg-raising inference is not valid with "bie". Due to this particular sensitivity to negation, it is difficult to determine whether the entry of "think" for "xiang" allows for neg-raising or not[25].

(32) Imperative negating "xiang"

Ni bie juede zhe hen jiandan
You -NEG think this very easy

'Don't think it is easy.'
$\not\to$ Think it is not easy.

Semantic shift Figure 3 illustrated the semantic shifts that occur when negation interacts with two meaning entries of the "xiang" (represented by the upper and lower arrows, corresponding to "think" and "want" respectively). Specifically, two meaning shifts are observed: from "want ¬ P" to "think ¬ P" and from "¬ think P" to "¬ want P," when the negator is "bu". It is important to mention that this section only provides descriptive information rather than a comprehensive explanation.

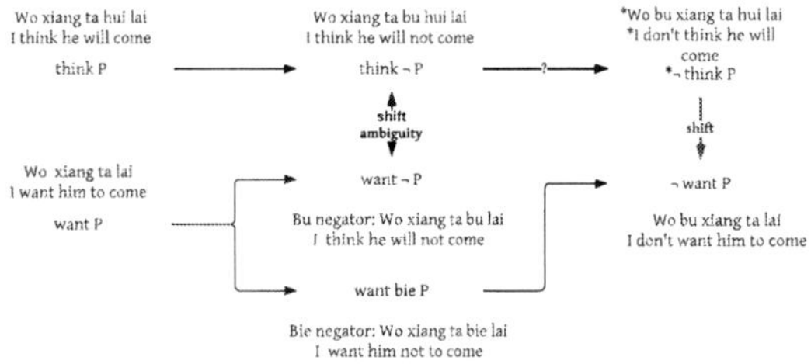

Figure 3: Semantic shift between "want" and "think"; the default negator is "bu" if there is no specification.

Figure 3 also reveals several possibilities of the failure of "¬ think P" (i.e., the neg-raising inference). First and most straightforward, the neg-raising does not happen, the negation is base-generated in the matrix clause. It is due to sensitivity to negation that "think" shifts to "want". As a by-product of this meaning shift, the auxiliary "hui" (will) is discarded because "will" and "want" are overlapping in terms of their meaning (i.e., showing future-orientation). However, this explanation faces a problem as it fails to account for why its "want" entry can have neg-raising inference. Second, neg-raising may have happened, but in the meantime, "think" changes its meaning to "want" due to negation. Third, there exists an potential meaning ambiguity between "think ¬ P" and "want ¬ P" under "bu" negation. The potential neg-raising may proceed though the "want" entry instead of the "think" entry. However, the last explanation is also unsatisfactory. For example, why does the ambiguity not work in the opposite way. Apart from that, the last possibility needs an account for the potential negator shift in " want ¬ P" (from "bu" to "bie" and then back to "bu" again).

6 Conclusion

"Xiang" shows that the stativity of vP plays a role in clausal complement selection and this is consistent with what is found with the English verb "think". This, however, is subject to many challenges, for instance, the stativity tests are limited in many ways (e.g., small in number), the existence of certain aspectual markers and modals inside the complement may influence the acceptability (20a,20b)[26]. Due to this, the conclusion that "xiang P" can only be stative may face potential challenges in the future. Given the three possibilities that lead to the failure of neg-raising, it is reasonable to maintain the potential neg-raising assumption, which is just blocked by the meaning shift due to negation. Hence "xiang" does not pose a real problem to Özyıldız (2021). The semantic shift in "xiang" is still insufficiently explained, given the focus of the paper is "xiang(think)" and its CP complement. I leave it to future research to elucidate the underlying factors that give rise to this meaning shift.

7 Acknowledgements

I am grateful to Kajsa Djärv for introducing me to the topic and providing valuable guidance. I would also like to extend my thanks to the two anonymous reviewers whose comments were clear and encouraging. Lastly, I thank my informants

[24]Here, I avoid using "xiang"(want) as an example because "want" shifts meaning under imperatives. In the meantime, I found out that the negators sometimes may not be the same before and after raising. "I -Bu want him to come." → "I want him -Bie/*Bu to come."

[25]My supervisor, Kajsa Djärv, also suggested that the observations made in non-neg-raising "xiang P" might undermine the applicability of Theiler et al.'s explanation for "*xiang Q" (canonically). However, the data presented by Özyıldız has already demonstrated that Theiler et al.'s account faces issues when applied to "think Q." Nevertheless, one question that arises is why we observe a pattern in English where the interpretation of the expression "¬ think" is neg-raising with P-complements varies based on whether it is stative or eventive, while in Mandarin, "¬ think" is consistently understood as "want," irrespective of stativity.

[26]cf.(20a): *I think-prog how to cook-perf or *I think-prog how to cook-LE, but "-perf" and "LE" seem to be good as in (20b). This can be syntactic constraints on finiteness as well.

and the members of the guided research group for their insightful questions and native knowledge.

References

Dorit Abusch. 2014. Temporal succession and aspectual type in visual narrative. *The Art and Craft of Semantics: A Festschrift for Irene Heim*, 1:9–29.

Yung-O Biq. 1989. Metalinguistic negation in mandarin. *Journal of Chinese Linguistics*, 17(1):75–95.

Yung-O Biq. 1991. The multiple uses of the second person singular pronoun ni in conversational mandarin. *Journal of Pragmatics*, 16(4):307–321.

Tatiana Bondarenko. 2020. Factivity from preexistence: Evidence from barguzin buryat. *Glossa: a journal of general linguistics*, 5(1).

Hongyuan Dong. 2018. *Semantics of Chinese questions: An interface approach*. Routledge.

David R Dowty. 1979. 5 dative'movement'and thomason's extensions of montague grammar. In *Linguistics, philosophy, and Montague grammar*, pages 153–222. University of Texas Press.

David R Dowty. 1986. The effects of aspectual class on the temporal structure of discourse: semantics or pragmatics? *Linguistics and philosophy*, pages 37–61.

Paul Egré. 2008. Question-embedding and factivity. *Grazer Philosophische Studien*, 77(1):85–125.

Thomas Ernst. 1995. Negation in mandarin chinese. *Natural Language & Linguistic Theory*, 13(4):665–707.

Lelia Glass. 2020. The negatively biased mandarin belief verb yǐwéi. *Studia Linguistica*.

Jane Grimshaw. 1979. Complement selection and the lexicon. *Linguistic inquiry*, 10(2):279–326.

Baozhang He. 1992. *Situation types and aspectual classes of verbs in Mandarin Chinese*. The Ohio State University.

Jaakko Hintikka. 1975. 'different constructions in terms of the basic epistemological verbs: A survey of some problems and proposals.

Paloma Jeretic and Deniz Özyıldız. 2022. Why neg-raising requires stativity. In *Amsterdam Colloquium*.

Lauri Karttunen. 1977. Syntax and semantics of questions. *Linguistics and philosophy*, 1:3–44.

Utpal Lahiri et al. 2002. *Questions and answers in embedded contexts*, volume 2. Oxford University Press on Demand.

George Lakoff. 1966. Stative adjectives and verbs in english.

Alex Lascarides and Nicholas Asher. 1993. Temporal interpretation, discourse relations and commonsense entailment. *Linguistics and philosophy*, 16(5):437–493.

Shuxiang Lü. 1999. *Xiandai Hanyu Babai Ci[800 Words in Modern Chinese]*. The Comercial Press.

Mari Broman Olsen. 1994. The semantics and pragmatics of lexical aspect features. *Studies in the linguistic sciences*.

Deniz Özyıldız. 2021. The event structure of attitudes.

Tom Roberts. 2019. I can't believe it's not lexical: Deriving distributed veridicality. In *Semantics and Linguistic Theory*, volume 29, pages 665–685.

Benjamin Spector and Paul Egré. 2015. A uniform semantics for embedded interrogatives: An answer, not necessarily the answer. *Synthese*, 192:1729–1784.

Nadine Theiler, Floris Roelofsen, and Maria Aloni. 2018. A uniform semantics for declarative and interrogative complements. *Journal of Semantics*, 35(3):409–466.

Nadine Theiler, Floris Roelofsen, and Maria Aloni. 2019. Picky predicates: Why believe doesn't like interrogative complements, and other puzzles. *Natural Language Semantics*, 27:95–134.

Wataru Uegaki. 2015. *Interpreting questions under attitudes*. Ph.D. thesis, Massachusetts Institute of Technology.

Wataru Uegaki. 2019. The semantics of question-embedding predicates. *Language and Linguistics Compass*, 13(1):e12308.

Yimei Xiang. 2013. Neg-raising and aspect: Evidence from mandarin. *University of Pennsylvania Working Papers in Linguistics*, 19(1):29.

Richard Xiao and Tony McEnery. 2004. *Aspect in Mandarin Chinese: A corpus-based study*, volume 73. John Benjamins Publishing.

Richard Z Xiao and Anthony M McEnery. 2008. Negation in chinese: a corpus-based study. *Journal of Chinese linguistics*, 36(2):274–330.

Bangjun Xu, Jingxiang Yin, Yi Qin, and Qiwang Hu. 2013. Semantic-syntactic description of chinese psycho-verb xiang. In *Chinese Lexical Semantics: 14th Workshop, CLSW 2013, Zhengzhou, China, May 10-12, 2013. Revised Selected Papers 14*, pages 10–18. Springer.

The indefinite-interrogative affinity in sign languages: the case of Catalan Sign Language

Raquel Veiga Busto and **Floris Roelofsen**
University of Amsterdam
{r.veigabusto,f.roelofsen}@uva.nl

Alexandra Navarrete-González
Universitat Pompeu Fabra
alexandra.navarrete@upf.edu

Abstract

Prior studies on spoken languages have shown that indefinite and interrogative pronouns may be formally very similar. Our research aims to understand if sign languages exhibit this type of affinity. This paper presents an overview of the phenomenon and reports on the results of two studies: a cross-linguistic survey based on a sample of 30 sign languages and an empirical investigation conducted with three deaf consultants of Catalan Sign Language (LSC). Our research shows that, in sign languages, certain signs have both existential and interrogative readings and it identifies the environments that make existential interpretations available in LSC.

1 Introduction

Research on spoken languages has shown that indefinite pronouns are commonly derived from generic nouns such as 'thing' or 'time' (as in English *something* or *sometime*) and the numeral 'one' (e.g., *someone* in English, *qualcuno* in Italian). Furthermore, indefinite pronouns may be morphologically very similar or even identical to interrogative pronouns (Haspelmath, 1997). For example, the Mandarin Chinese form *shenme* ('something'/'what') has both indefinite and interrogative functions and the English indefinite *anywhere* is somehow linked to the interrogative word *where* and the indefiniteness marker *any-*. This formal resemblance is known as the indefinite-interrogative affinity (Bhat, 2004; Gartner, 2009; Onea, 2021).

In his typology of spoken language indefinites, Haspelmath (1997) made the following observation: when indefinite and interrogative pronouns are formally similar but not fully identical, the indefinite is always the element that is more morphologically complex. That is, there is a universal asymmetric markedness relation such that interrogative pronouns are virtually never more marked than indefinite pronouns nor derived from them.[1] This is why indefinite pronouns bearing a formal resemblance with interrogative words are commonly referred to as interrogative-based indefinites (Haspelmath, 1997) or as *wh*-indefinites (Bruening, 2007). Depending on their form, *wh*-indefinites may be further broken down into two categories: bare, if their form is identical to that of the interrogative, and complex, if they involve the interrogative along with some additional morphology. Languages differ with respect to the type of affinity they allow: some languages have both bare and complex *wh*-indefinites, some languages have one type only, and yet others do not show this type of affinity (cf. Yun, 2013).

In this paper, we will follow Hengeveld et al. (2022) and adopt the term *quexistentials* to refer to those elements that may be used either as question words or as existential indefinites. Likewise, we will refer to the interrogative interpretation of a quexistential as *qu of quex* and to the existential reading of the quexistential as *ex of quex*. While in its original formulation, the term applies only to those words that allow interrogative and indefinite uses without differences in spell-out, we will extend the definition to cover those cases in which the two uses correspond to similar but not fully identical forms. The main motivation is that interrogative and indefinite signs tend to co-occur with specific sets of non-manual markers (NMMs), but we do not yet know what the exact role of such markers is nor whether fully identical forms can be found in any sign language. Therefore, we will use the term *quexistential* when the manual sign is the same and the NMNs differ, but also when the manual sign is not fully identical in both readings, either because it combines with other signs or because it involves a change on its phonological make-up (e.g., by

[1] Similar observations are found in Moravcsik (1969) and Ultan (1969).

Proceedings of the 4th Workshop on Inquisitiveness Below and Beyond the Sentence Boundary (InqBnB4), pages 50–60
June 20, 2023.

means of reduplication or movement modification). To make these distinctions explicit, we will use the labels *bare* and *complex quexistential*.

Despite claims that in some sign languages certain items may function both as indefinite and as interrogative pronouns, the extent to which the indefinite-interrogative affinity is found in the visual modality has not yet been investigated (Zeshan, 2006a; Cormier, 2012; Zeshan and Palfreyman, 2017). Thus, it is also not clear whether Haspelmath's universal, according to which indefinite pronouns always constitute derived forms, can be taken to hold for sign languages as well. Indeed, this is the main reason for adopting the term *quexistentials*, as it remains neutral with respect to the nature of the interrogative-indefinite affinity (i.e., it does not presume that the indefinite is always derived from the interrogative).

In this paper, we aim to investigate the extent to which the indefinite-interrogative affinity is found in the signed modality. The roadmap of the paper is as follows. Section 2 provides an overview of the distribution of quexistentials across spoken and signed languages. In Section 3, we zoom in on the morphology of quexistentials and the distribution of the ex of quex in Catalan Sign Language (LSC). Section 4 summarizes our findings and Section 5 suggests directions for future research. The main contribution of this study is that it provides the first description of the morphology and the distribution of the ex of quex in a sign language.

2 Cross-linguistic distribution of the indefinite-interrogative affinity

The indefinite-interrogative affinity is a widespread phenomenon among the world's spoken languages. Importantly, this affinity is not restricted to a specific language family or to a particular geographic area. In Ultan's (1969) typology of interrogative systems, it is attested in 77 out a sample of 79 spoken languages. In Haspelmath's typology of indefinite pronouns (1997), 63 out of a sample of 100 spoken languages were found to show this type of affinity.

2.1 Distribution of the ex of quex

The distinction between bare and complex quexistentials has been claimed to impact the licensing conditions of the ex of quex. According to Yun (2013), complex forms do not exhibit any syntactic or semantic restriction, thus patterning with non-quexistential indefinites.

Bare quexistentials, by contrast, are subject to different constraints across languages. While the contexts in which the existential reading of bare quexistentials arises are not uniform, in many languages, the ex of quex occurs in environments that license NPIs. Let's take the case of Mandarin Chinese as an illustration. In Mandarin Chinese, the ex of quex is licensed by modals (1), negation (2), antecedents of conditionals (3) and polar questions (4). Other licensors include imperatives and future markers, non-factive predicates like *renwei* 'think' and the universal quantificational particle *dou* (Lin, 1998; Chen, 2018; Yang et al., 2022). Crucially, the ex of quex may also occur in environments that do not license NPIs, such as positive sentences marked with progressive or perfective aspect (Chen, 2018; Liu and Yang, 2021). When occurring in such contexts, the forms are argued to convey speaker's ignorance about the identity of the individual that satisfies the description of the *wh*-phrase, as in (5) (examples are adapted from Chen, 2018, 142–143).

(1) Ni bixu chi dian **shenme**
You must eat CL QUEX
'You must eat something.'

(2) Zhangsan mei chi **shenme** dongxi
Zhangsan NEG eat QUEX thing
'Zhangsan didn't eat anything.'

(3) Ruguo ni you **shenme** wenti, jiu lai wen wo
If you have QUEX question, then come ask me
'If you have any question, come and ask me.'

(4) Zhangsan chi-le **shenme** ma?
Zhangsan eat-ASP QUEX Q?
Did Zhangsan eat anything?

(5) Zhangsan mai le dian **shenme** song gei Lisi
Zhangsan buy Asp CL QUEX give to Lisi
'Zhangsan bought something for Lisi (the speaker does not know specifically what he bought).'

Finally, some languages may restrict the position in which the ex of quex is allowed. For example, in Dutch and German, it must occur inside the verb phrase, and it cannot be scrambled outside the VP without losing its indefinite interpretation (Postma, 1994).

2.2 The indefinite-interrogative affinity in sign languages

In order to investigate whether sign languages show the same kind of affinity between question words and existential indefinites, we first conducted a survey based on a convenience sample of 30 different sign languages. The data gathered consisted mainly of articles and book chapters (most about interrogatives, with only a few addressing indefinite pronouns), as well as online dictionaries and grammars. Crucially, the languages in our sample were selected based on the availability of the data only, and no further factors were considered at this point.

2.3 Results

We found that the indefinite-interrogative affinity is attested in 11 out of the 30 sign languages considered in our sample. For the remaining 19 languages, either the affinity was claimed not to exist or no information on the topic was available. The list of sign languages and the semantic categories that allow both interrogative and indefinite uses are presented in Table 1. The complete list of languages is presented in Appendix A.

Despite being heavily biased towards European sign languages, our sample show that the indefinite-interrogative affinity is attested in different geographic areas. Note, however, that languages such as BSL, Auslan and NZSL are historically related. Therefore, identification of the same types of quexistentials across this group of languages is not entirely unexpected.

Overall, our survey reveals that the person category quexistential, which covers the existential reading ('someone') and the interrogative interpretation ('who'), is the most common across sign languages. However, since in most cases discussion of the features was rather superficial, no detailed comparison of the distribution of quexistentials in sign languages could be carried out. In fact, from the data available it could not be established whether or not quexistentials referring to semantic categories other than person, thing and location were possible in the sign languages in our sample. In the case of NS and Libras, there is simply no indication about the categories in which quexistentials are allowed. This is why the two languages are marked with a star in Table 1.[2]

With some notable exceptions, such as Barberà et al. (2018) for LSC, the contexts that license existential interpretations are not explicitly identified either. That said, for UgSL it is noted that the use of the ex of quex is not possible across the board (cf. Lutalo-Kiingi, 2014, 232). Taking this into consideration, we decided to conduct fieldwork so as to i) maximize the diversity of our sample; and ii) collect more detailed, comparable data from specific sign languages. The next section describes the case of LSC, which is the first sign language we studied and the one in which we piloted our research methodology.

3 Quexistentials in LSC

LSC is a language argued to have a bare quexistential in the person category, which can mean either 'who' or 'someone', as well as two complex quexistentials, the compounds QUEX:person^QUEX:quantity and QUEX:person^IX$_{3pl}$,[3] meaning 'someone' (Barberà and Quer, 2013; Barberà, 2016; Barberà and Cabredo Hofherr, 2018; Barberà, 2021).[4] According to (Barberà, 2021), the existential reading of the bare quexistential is licensed by the NMMs used in contexts of indefiniteness, which in LSC include sucking the cheeks in, pulling the corners of the mouth down, and sometimes a shrug (Barberà, 2015).[5,6]

3.1 Method

In order to investigate if quexistentials are equally productive in other semantic categories and to determine their distribution in the language, we con-

[2]In fact, the case of Libras is further complicated by the fact that while Zeshan (2004) claims that question words may have indefinite uses, a later study by Quadros (2006) states the opposite.

[3]Following standard conventions, manual signs are glossed in small capitals. The gloss QUEX:'category' represents quexistentials and the semantic category they belong to. Multimorphemic signs are glossed using a circumflex accent between the morphemes (SIGN^SIGN). The gloss IX stands for pointing signs, -rep stands for reduplication and number subscripts represent person values. When more than one word is needed to gloss the meaning of a sign, the words are separated by dashes (e.g., HOW_MANY corresponds to a single sign in LSC). Classifiers are glossed as CL:'meaning of the classifier'.

[4]In these publications, complex quexistentials are glossed as WHO^SOME and WHO^IX$_{3pl}$.

[5]The NMMs used in indefinite contexts, just like the ones used in interrogative contexts, are subject to cross-linguistic variation (Barberà and Cormier, 2017). For example, unlike the case of LSC, the NMMs of indefiniteness reported for ASL are wrinkled nose, furrowed brows, and a rapid head shake (Bahan, 1996).

[6]For NZSL, McKee (2006, 80) claims that the quexistential interpretation is differentiated by context, mouthing patterns, and the presence or absence of interrogative NMMs.

Language	Acronym	QUEX:person	QUEX:location	QUEX:thing
Australian Sign Language	Auslan	✓	✓	–
Brazilian Sign Language	Libras	*	*	*
British Sign Language	BSL	✓	✓	–
Catalan Sign Language	LSC	✓	–	–
Finnish Sign Language	SVK	✓	✓	✓
Japanese Sign Language	NS	*	*	*
Kenian Sign Language	KSL	✓	–	–
New Zealand Sign Language	NZSL	✓	✓	–
Russian Sign Language	RSL	✓	–	–
Spanish Sign Language	LSE	✓	–	–
Ugandan Sign Language	UgSL	✓	–	–

Table 1: Quexistentials in sign languages.

ducted elicitation sessions with three deaf LSC consultants.

Since interrogative signs have already been described in prior LSC studies (Quer et al., 2005; Alba, 2016; Cañas Peña, 2020), no specific task was carried out to elicit the forms. The inventory of question words commonly listed in previous literature is presented in Figures 1 to 10.

Figure 1: WHO

Figure 2: WHAT

Figure 3: WHEN.past

Figure 4: WHEN.fut

Figure 5: WHERE

Figure 6: HOW_MANY

Figure 7: REASON

Figure 8: WHY

Figure 9: WHICH

Figure 10: HOW

To establish the inventory of indefinite pronouns and identify the contexts in which the ex of quex is possible in LSC, we develop a questionnaire aimed at eliciting indefinite pronouns referring to the same ontological categories observed in the interrogative paradigm, namely: person, thing, time, location, quantity, cause, determiner and manner. For each semantic category, we elicit indefinite pronouns in environments known to influence the choice of the indefinite form (see Section 2.1). Specifically, we elicited indefinites in the scope of possibility and necessity modals (epistemic and deontic), in polar questions, in the antecedent of conditionals, in affirmative episodic sentences and in the context of negation. The remainder of this section describes our main results.

3.2 Results

The indefinite paradigm

As it has been observed for many other languages, indefinite pronouns in LSC may be formally similar to generic nouns (e.g., SOMETHING^PERSON 'someone'), the numeral ONE (e.g., ONE^SOMETHING 'something') and question words (e.g., QUEX:person^ANY 'anyone'). However, indefinites that combine two of these strategies are fairly common as well (DAY^ONE 'sometime', ONE^PERSON/QUEX:person^PERSON-rep 'someone').

Quexistentials: distribution

- Apart from the person category, which is the only one that has been previously described for LSC, we found that the ex of quex is also possible in the categories time, quantity and cause.

- There are four non-quexistential interrogatives (i.e., question words that do not allow for indefinite uses). These correspond to the signs in Figures 2, 5, 9 and 10, which translate roughly as 'what', 'where', 'which' and 'how' in English. Given that sentences containing these signs do not allow for an existential interpretation, they are considered ungrammatical in non-interrogative constructions (see (6) and (7)).

(6) *DISAPPEAR **WHAT**, GUILT IX$_2$
Intended: 'If something disappears, you will be held responsible.'

(7) *IX$_1$ MUST DRUG **WHICH** MONEY^BUY
Intended: 'I must buy some medicines.'

- The existential reading of quexistentials is licensed in the same environments for all four semantic categories. That is, it is possible in polar questions, in the antecedent of conditionals, in positive episodic sentences and under modals (see Table 2).[7,8] These environments are illustrated in sentences (8) to (11) below. Examples (8-a) to (11-a) correspond to the person category quexistential; examples (8-b) to (11-b) correspond to quexistentials of the semantic category quantity.

(8) Polar question:
  a. COME **QUEX:person**?
  'Has anyone come?'
  b. IX$_2$ SEE PLANET **QUEX:quantity**?
  'Have you seen any planets?'

(9) Antecedent of a conditional:
  a. COME **QUEX:person**, IX$_1$ TAKE_CARE
  'If someone comes, I'll take care.'
  b. IX$_2$ DISCOVER **QUEX:quantity**, LET_KNOW$_1$
  'If you discover something, let me know.'

(10) Episodic:
  a. YESTERDAY SUBWAY **QUEX:person** LOOK$_1$-rep
  'Someone kept looking at me yesterday at the subway.'
  b. BOY^CHILD SEE **QUEX:quantity**
  'The child saw some.PL.'

(11) Modal:
  a. SEEM OUTSIDE **QUEX:person**
  'There appears to be someone outside.'
  b. TRAFFIC SIGN-rep IX **QUEX:quantity** MUST UPGRADE-rep NEW CL:'put'-rep
  'Some traffic signs must be replaced.'

- Except for the sign REASON, the ex of quex is not possible under negation. This is shown in (12), where the general negative non-quexistential indefinite NOTHING-o is used instead of QUEX:person. For ease of illustration, the two signs are presented in Figures 11 and 12.

(12) Negation:
COME **NOTHING-o**
'Nobody came.'

---

[7] Since judgments were uniform for the different modals considered in this study, Table 2 collapses deontic necessity, deontic possibility, epistemic necessity and epistemic possibility modals into the heading "Modals".

[8] Results for the category cause correspond to the judgments obtained for the sign REASON only. Judgments for the sign WHY were not as robust and they will be tested again in a follow-up study.

Category	Polar question	Antecedent of a conditional	Positive episodic sentence	Negation	Modals
Person	✓	✓	✓	–	✓
Thing	–	–	–	–	–
Quantity	✓	✓	✓	–	✓
Location	–	–	–	–	–
Time	✓	✓	✓	–	✓
Manner	–	–	–	–	–
Determiner	–	–	–	–	–
Cause	✓	✓	✓	✓	✓

Table 2: Quexistentials in LSC.

Figure 11: QUEX:person

Figure 12: NOTHING-o

Quexistentials: morphology

- Depending on the semantic category and the context in which they are used, both bare and complex quexistentials are possible. In the existential reading, the quexistentials corresponding to the categories person, time and quantity may appear either bare or in combination with other signs. Again, the sign REASON differs from the rest in that it always needs to combine with other sign(s) in its existential reading.

- To give an example, while sentences (8-a) to (11-a) contain bare quexistentials only, complex quexistentials could also occur in the same environments. As shown in Table 3, there is only one exception to this: in the person category, deontic possibility modals seem to always require a complex quexistential (e.g., QUEX:person^ANY or QUEX:person^IX-b, as in (13)). Interestingly, a combination of two quexistentials is also possible, as shown in (14) below. Furthermore, the quexistential QUEX:quantity, which covers both the categories of people and things, may also be used in the same context instead of QUEX:person, and generate the same free choice inference, see (15). For ease of comparison, the examples provide video recorded sentences as well. They can be accessed by clicking on the hands icon next to the example sentence.

(13) IX$_2$ CAN CONTACT QUEX:person^IX-b
'You can talk to anyone.'

(14) IX$_2$ CAN CONTACT QUEX:person^QUEX:quantity
'You can talk to anyone.'

(15) NO, IX$_2$ CAN CONTACT ANY^QUEX: quantity
'No, you can talk to anyone.'

Environment	Bare quex	Complex quex
Polar question	✓	✓
Epistemic necessity	✓	✓
Epistemic possibility	✓	✓
Deontic necessity	✓	✓
Deontic possibility	–	✓
Conditional's antecedent	✓	✓
Negation	–	–
Episodic	✓	✓

Table 3: Distribution of bare and complex quex in the person category.

- Finally, it must be noted that for the quexistential indefinite to be used, the identity of the referent must be unknown to the speaker (see also Barberà (2015) and Barberà et al. (2018)).

4 Conclusion

The results of our study show the indefinite-interrogative affinity is a phenomenon attested across different sign languages. Besides, our investigation shows that, in LSC, quexistentials are possible in different semantic categories and that the distribution of the ex of quex follows a pattern similar to the one described for spoken languages such as Mandarin Chinese. In particular, the existential reading of quexistentials is licensed in, at least, the following contexts: polar questions, epistemic and deontic modals, antecedents of conditionals and positive episodic sentences.

5 Future work

Despite having demonstrated that certain contexts require complex quexistentials for the existential interpretation to arise, we cannot yet conclude that Haspelmath's universal, according to which indefinites are always more morphologically complex than interrogatives, necessarily applies to the case of LSC. To be able to reach that conclusion, we would also have to compare the articulation of bare quexistentials when they are interpreted as question words vs. when they are interpreted as existential indefinites. In this respect, prior findings from some of the sign languages considered in the survey presented in Section 2.3 may shed some light on this question. In some sign languages, signs that have both interrogative and non-interrogative uses tend to differ in the movement parameter, such that the interrogative reading commonly takes a repetitive movement (Zeshan, 2004; Zeshan and Palfreyman, 2017). Interestingly, similar strategies have been reported for spoken language indefinites. For example, indefinite markers might consist of an affix, a particle or a sequence of particles. Crucially, they might also consist of reduplication and stem modification (Haspelmath, 1997). This would entail that the interrogative would be the more morphologically complex member of the pair in some sign languages, as opposed to what is claimed in Haspelmath's universal for spoken languages.

As mentioned earlier, NMMs may, by themselves, differentiate the two readings that quexistentials may have. However, the possible combinations of NMMs and their exact scope in the sentence have not yet been addressed in detail in this investigation. Besides, the very nature of our research questions crucially depends on collecting and comparing data from other sign languages as well. These issues will be addressed in future research.

Acknowledgments

We gratefully acknowledge financial support from the Netherlands Organization for Scientific Research (NWO, grant number VI.C.201.014). We are grateful to our Catalan Sign Language consultants Delfina Aliaga, Santiago Frigola and David Falguera, as well as to the two anonymous reviewers of this paper for their feedback.

References

Enoch Aboh, Roland Pfau, and Ulrike Zeshan. 2005. When a wh-word is not a wh-word: the case of Indian Sign Language. In Tanmoy Bhattacharya, editor, *The Yearbook of South Asian languages and linguistics*, pages 11–43. Mouton de Gruyter, Berlin.

P. Akach. 1991. *Kenyan Sign Language Dictionary*. Kenyan National Association of the Deaf, Nairobi.

Cèlia Alba. 2016. *Wh-Questions in Catalan Sign Language*. Ph.D. thesis, Pompeu Fabra University, Barcelona.

Benjamin J. Bahan. 1996. *Nonmanual realization of agreement in American Sign Language*. Ph.D. thesis, Boston University, Boston, MA.

Charlotte Lee Baker-Shenk. 1983. *A microanalysis of the nonmanual components of questions in American Sign Language*. Ph.D. thesis, University of California, Berkeley.

Gemma Barberà. 2015. *The meaning of space in sign language. Reference, specificity and structure in Catalan Sign Language discourse*. Mouton de Gruyter & Ishara Press, Berlin/Boston.

Gemma Barberà. 2016. Indefiniteness and specificity marking in Catalan Sign Language (LSC). *Sign Language & Linguistics*, 19(1):1–36.

Gemma Barberà. 2021. Specificity and definiteness. In Josep Quer, Roland Pfau, and Annika Herrmann, editors, *The Routledge Handbook of Theoretical and Experimental Sign Language Research*, pages 403–422. Routledge, London.

Gemma Barberà and Patricia Cabredo Hofherr. 2018. Two indefinite pronouns in Catalan Sign Language (LSC). In *Proceedings of Sinn und Bedeutung 21*, pages 89–106. University of Edinburgh.

Gemma Barberà, Patricia Cabredo Hofherr, and Josep Quer. 2018. Agent-backgrounding in Catalan Sign Language (LSC). *Sign Language & Linguistics*, 21(2):334–348.

Gemma Barberà and Kearsy Cormier. 2017. Reference. In Josep Quer, Carlo Cecchetto, Caterina Donati, Carlo Geraci, Meltem Kelepir, Roland Pfau, and Markus Steinbach, editors, *SignGram blueprint: A guide to sign language grammar writing*, pages 670–680. De Gruyter Mouton, Berlin.

Gemma Barberà and Josep Quer. 2013. Impersonal reference in Catalan Sign Language (LSC). In Laurence Meurant, Aurélie Sinte, Mieke Van Herreweghe, and Myriam Vermeerberge, editors, *Sign language research uses and practices: Crossing views on theoretical and applied sign language linguistics*, pages 237–258. Ishara Press and de Gruyter Mouton, Berlin/Boston.

Darbhe Narayana Shankara Bhat. 2004. The indefinite-interrogative puzzle. In *Pronouns*, pages 226–249. Oxford University Press, Oxford.

Felicia Bisnath. 2021. Wh-questions in the Trinidad and Tobago signing community. In *Proceedings of the Fifty-sixth Annual Meeting of the Chicago Linguistic Society*, pages 37–50. Chicago Linguistic Society.

Denis Bouchard and Colette Dubuisson. 1995. Grammar, order and position of wh-signs in Québec Sign Language. *Sign Language Studies*, 87:99–139.

Chiara Branchini and Lara Mantovan. 2020. *A grammar of Italian Sign Language (LIS)*. Edizioni Ca' Foscari, Venice.

Benjamin Bruening. 2007. *Wh*-in-situ does not correlate with *wh*-indefinites or question particles. *Linguistic Inquiry*, 38:139–166.

Sara Cañas Peña. 2020. Syntax: 1.2. Interrogatives. In Josep Quer and Gemma Barberà, editors, *A Grammar of Catalan Sign Language (LSC)*. SIGN-HUB Sign Language Grammar Series.

Pietro Celo. 1996. Linguistic and pragmatic aspects of the interrogative form in Italian Sign Language. In Ceil Lucas, editor, *Multicultural aspects of sociolinguistics in deaf communities*, pages 132–151. Gallaudet University Press, Washington, DC.

Yijun Chen. 2012. *Questioning in Taiwan Sign Language Conversation*. Ph.D. thesis, National Chung Cheng University, Chiayi.

Zhuo Chen. 2018. *Wh*-indefinites are dependent indefinites: a study on *shenme*. In *Proceedings of the 35th West Coast Conference on Formal Linguistics*, pages 142–150. Somerville, MA: Cascadilla Proceedings Project.

Jane Coerts. 1990. The analysis of interrogatives and negations in Sign Language of the Netherland. In *Current trends in European Sign Language Research: Proceedings of the Third European Congress on Sign Language Research*, pages 265–277. Signum.

Jane Coerts. 1992. *Nonmanual grammatical markers: An analysis of interrogatives, negations and topicalisations in Sign Language of the Netherlands*. Ph.D. thesis, University of Amsterdam.

Frances Conlin, Paul Hagstrom, and Carol Neidle. 2003. A particle of indefiniteness in American Sign Language. *Linguistic Discovery*, 2:1–21.

Kearsy Cormier. 2012. Pronouns. In Roland Pfau, Markus Steinbach, and Bencie Woll, editors, *Sign language: An international handbook*, pages 227–244. Mouton de Gruyter, Berlin.

Miroslava Cruz Aldrete. 2008. *Gramática de la Lengua de Señas Mexicana*. Ph.D. thesis, Colegio de México.

Hasan Dikyuva, Bahtiyar Makaroğlu, and Engin Arık. 2017. *Turkish Sign Language grammar*. Ministry of Family and Social Policies Press, Ankara.

Colette Dubuisson, Johanne Boulanger, Jules Desrosiers, and Linda Lelièvre. 1991. Les mouvements de tête dans les interrogatives en langue des signes québécoise. *Revue québécoise de linguistique*, 20(2):93–121.

Jordan Fenlon, Kearsy Cormier, Ramas Rentelis, Adam Schembri, Katherine Rowley, Robert Adam, and Bencie Woll. 2014. *BSL SignBank: A lexical database of British Sign Language*. Deafness, Cognition and Language Research Centre, University College London, London. 1st Edition.

Ana María Fernández Soneira. 2008. *La cantidad a manos llenas. La expresión de la cuantificación en la lengua de signos española*. Fundación CNSE, Madrid.

Finnish Association of the Deaf. 2003. *Suvi–Suomalaisen Viittomakielen Verkkosanakirja [The online dictionary of Finnish Sign Language]*.

Susan Fischer. 2006. Questions and Negation in American Sign Language. In Ulrike Zeshan, editor, *Interrogative and Negative Constructions in Sign Languages*, pages 165–197. Ishara Press, Nijmegen.

Hans-Martin Gartner. 2009. More on the indefinite-interrogative affinity: The view from embedded non-finite interrogatives. *Linguistic Typology*, 13(1):1–37.

Carlo Geraci, Robert Bayley, Anna Cardinaletti, Carlo Cecchetto, and Caterina Donati. 2015. Variation in Italian Sign Language (LIS): The case of *wh*-signs. *Linguistics*, 53(1):125–151.

Aslı Göksel and Meltem Kelepir. 2013. The phonological and semantic bifurcation of the functions of an articulator: HEAD in questions in Turkish Sign Language. *Sign Language and Linguistics*, 16(1):1–30.

Martin Haspelmath. 1997. *Indefinite pronouns*. Oxford University Press, Oxford.

Kees Hengeveld, Sabine Iatridou, and Floris Roelofsen. 2022. Quexistentials and focus. *Linguistic Inquiry*, pages 1–54.

Ángel Luis Herrero Blanco. 2009. *Gramática didáctica de la lengua de signos española (LSE)*. Ediciones SM, Madrid.

Julie A. Hochgesang, Onno Crasborn, and Diane Lillo-Martin. 2018. *ASL Signbank*. Haskins Lab, Yale University, New Haven, CT.

Trevor Johnston. 2001. The lexical database of Auslan (Australian Sign Language). *Sign Language & Linguistics*, 4(1/2):145–169.

Trevor Johnston and Adam Schembri. 2007. *Australian Sign Language: An introduction to sign language linguistics*. Cambridge University Press, Cambridge.

Vadim Kimmelman. 2018. Impersonal reference in Russian Sign Language (RSL). *Sign Language and Linguistics*, 21(2):204–231.

Ulrika Klomp. 2021. *A descriptive grammar of Sign Language of the Netherlands*. Ph.D. thesis, University of Amsterdam.

Andrea Lackner. 2018. Interrogativity. In *Functions of head and body movements in Austrian Sign Language*, pages 139–170. De Gruyter Mouton, Berlin/Boston.

Hao Lin. 2019. Interrogative marking in Chinese Sign Language: A preliminary corpus-based investigation. *Sign language and Linguistics*, 22(2):241–266.

Jo-wang Lin. 1998. On existential polarity *wh*-phrases in Chinese. *Journal of East Asian Linguistics*, 7:219–255.

Mingming Liu and Yu'an Yang. 2021. Modal *wh*-indefinites in Mandarin. In *Proceedings of Sinn und Bedeutung 25*, pages 581–599. University College London and Queen Mary University of London.

Sam Lutalo-Kiingi. 2014. *A descriptive grammar of morphosyntactic constructions in Ugandan Sign Language (UgSL)*. Ph.D. thesis, University of Central Lancashire.

María Ignacia Massone. 1996. *Gramática y léxico de la lengua de señas argentina*. Ph.D. thesis, Universidad de Buenos Aires.

David McKee, Rachel McKee, Sara Pivac Alexander, Linette Pivac, and Mireille Vale. 2011. *Online dictionary of New Zealand Sign Language*. Deaf Studies Research Unit, Victoria University of Wellington, Wellington.

Rachel McKee. 2006. Aspects of interrogatives and negation in New Zealand Sign Language. In Ulrike Zeshan, editor, *Interrogative and Negative Constructions in Sign Languages*, pages 70–90. Ishara Press, Nijmegen.

Irit Meir. 2004. Question and Negation in Israeli Sign Language. *Sign Language and Linguistics*, 7(2):97–124.

Edith A. Moravcsik. 1969. Determination. In *Working papers on language universals, 1*, pages 63–98a. Stanford University Press, Stanford, CA.

Michael W. Morgan. 2006. Interrogatives and negatives in Japanese Sign Language. In Ulrike Zeshan, editor, *Interrogative and Negative Constructions in Sign Languages*, pages 91–127. Ishara Press, Nijmegen.

Carol Neidle. 2002. Language across modalities: ASL focus and question constructions. *Linguistic Variation Yearbook*, 2:71–98.

Angela M. Nonaka. 2010. Interrogatives in Ban Khor Sign Language: A preliminary description. In Gaurav Mathur and Donna Jo Napoli, editors, *Deaf around the world: The impact of language*, pages 194–220. Oxford University Press, Oxford.

Edgar Onea. 2021. Indefinite-interrogative affinity. In Daniel Gutzmann, Lisa Matthewson, Cecile Meier, Hotze Rullmann, and Thomas E. Zimmermann, editors, *The Wiley Blackwell Companion to Semantics, vol. 5*. Wiley-Blackwell, West Sussex.

Gertjan Postma. 1994. The indefinite reading of WH. *Linguistics in the Netherlands*, 11(1):187–198.

Ronice Müller de Quadros. 2006. Questions in Brazilian Sign Language (LSB). In Ulrike Zeshan, editor, *Interrogative and Negative Constructions in Sign Languages*, pages 270–283. Ishara Press, Nijmegen.

Josep (dir.) Quer, Eva M. Rondoni (dir. tècn.), Gemma Barberà, Santiago Frigola, Delfina Aliaga, Josep Boronat, Joan M. Gil, Pilar Iglesias, and Marina Martínez. 2005. *Gramàtica bàsica LSC*. FESOCA, DOMAD, Barcelona.

Leena Savolainen. 2006. Interrogatives and negatives in Finnish Sign Language: An overview. In Ulrike Zeshan, editor, *Interrogative and Negative Constructions in Sign Languages*, pages 284–302. Ishara Press, Nijmegen.

Katharina Schalber. 2006. What is the chin doing? An analysis of interrogatives in Austrian Sign Language. *Sign Language and Linguistics*, 9(1/2):133–150.

Hana Strachoňová. 2022. On question words in Czech Sign Language. *Sign Language and Linguistics*, 25(1):58–91.

Rachel Sutton-Spence and Bencie Woll. 1999. *The linguistics of British Sign Language: An introduction*. Cambridge University Press, Cambridge.

Yim-Binh Sze. 2000. *Space and nominals in Hong Kong Sign Language*. Ph.D. thesis, The Chinese University of Hong Kong.

Gladys Tang. 2006. Questions and Negation in Hong Kong Sign Language. In Ulrike Zeshan, editor, *Interrogative and Negative Constructions in Sign Languages*, pages 198–224. Ishara Press, Nijmegen.

Tegnspråksutvalget. 1988. *Norsk Tegnordbok [Norwegian Sign Dictionary]*. Bergen, Norway.

The University of Jyväskylä. 2018. Finnish Signbank. Available in the Language Bank of Finland.

Jane Tsay, James H.-Y. Tai, and Yijun Chen. 2015. *Taiwan Sign Language Online Dictionary*. Institute of Linguistics, National Chung Cheng University, Taiwan. 3rd Edition.

Russell Ultan. 1969. Some general characteristics of interrogative systems. In *Working papers on language universals, 1*, pages 41–63a. Stanford University Press, Stanford, CA.

Mieke Van Herreweghe and Myriam Vermeerbergen. 2006. Interrogatives and Negatives in Flemish Sign Language. In Ulrike Zeshan, editor, *Interrogative and Negative Constructions in Sign Languages*, pages 225–257. Ishara Press, Nijmegen.

Silvana C. Veinberg. 1993. La función lingüística de los rasgos no-manuales en la aseveración, la negación y la interrogación en la Lengua de Señas Argentina. *Signo y Seña*, 2:101–125.

Marit Vogt-Svendsen. 1990. Eye gaze in Norwegian Sign Language interrogatives. In *SLR '87: Papers from The Fourth International Symposium on Sign Language Research*, pages 153–162, Hamburg. Signum.

Yu'an Yang, Daniel Goodhue, Valentine Hacquard, and Jeffrey Lidz. 2022. Do children know *wh*anything? 3-year-olds know the ambiguity of *wh*-phrases in Mandarin. *Language Acquisition*, 29(3):296–326.

Jiwon Yun. 2013. Wh*-indefinites: meaning and prosody*. Ph.D. thesis, Cornell University.

Ulrike Zeshan. 2003. Indo-Pakistani Sign Language grammar: A typological outline. *Sign Language Studies*, 3:157–212.

Ulrike Zeshan. 2004. Interrogative constructions in signed languages: Crosslinguistic perspectives. *Language*, 80(1):7–39.

Ulrike Zeshan. 2006a. Negative and interrogative constructions in sign languages: A case study in sign language typology. In Ulrike Zeshan, editor, *Interrogative and Negative Constructions in Sign Languages*, pages 28–68. Ishara Press, Nijmegen.

Ulrike Zeshan. 2006b. Negative and interrogatives structures in Turkish Sign Language. In Ulrike Zeshan, editor, *Interrogative and Negative Constructions in Sign Languages*, pages 128–164. Ishara Press, Nijmegen.

Ulrike Zeshan. 2006c. Regional variation in Indo-Pakistani Sign Language: Evidence from content questions and negatives. In Ulrike Zeshan, editor, *Interrogative and Negative Constructions in Sign Languages*, pages 303–323. Ishara Press, Nijmegen.

Ulrike Zeshan and Nick Palfreyman. 2017. Sign language typology. In Alexandra Y. Aikhenvald and R. M. W. Dixon, editors, *The Cambridge Handbook of Linguistic Typology*, pages 178–216. Cambridge University Press, Nijmegen.

Ninoslava Šarac, Katharina Schalber, Tamara Alibašić, and Ronnie B. Wilbur. 2007. Crosslinguistic Comparison of Interrogatives in Croatian, Austrian and American Sign Languages. In Pamela Perniss, Roland Pfau, and Markus Steinbach, editors, *Visible variation: Comparative studies on sign language structure*, pages 207–244. Mouton de Gruyter, Berlin.

Ninoslava Šarac and Ronnie B. Wilbur. 2006. Interrogative structures in Croatian Sign Language: Polar and content questions. *Sign Language and Linguistics*, 9(1/2):151–167.

A List of sign languages

Sign Language name	Acronym	Sources
American Sign Language	ASL	Baker-Shenk (1983); Neidle (2002); Conlin et al. (2003); Fischer (2006); Hochgesang et al. (2018)
Argentine Sign Language	LSA	Veinberg (1993); Massone (1996)
Australian Sign Language	Auslan	Johnston (2001); Zeshan (2004) Johnston and Schembri (2007)
Austrian Sign Language	ÖGS	Schalber (2006); Šarac et al. (2007); Lackner (2018)
Ban Khor Sign Language	BKSL	Nonaka (2010)
Brazilian Sign Language	Libras	Zeshan (2004); Quadros (2006)
British Sign Language	BSL	Sutton-Spence and Woll (1999); Cormier (2012); Fenlon et al. (2014)
Catalan Sign Language	LSC	Alba (2016); Barberà (2016); Barberà and Cabredo Hofherr (2018); Barberà et al. (2018)
Chinese Sign Language	CSL	Lin (2019)
Croatian Sign Language	HZJ	Šarac and Wilbur (2006); Šarac et al. (2007)
Czech Sign Language	ČZJ	Strachoňová (2022)
Finnish Sign Language	SVK	Finnish Association of the Deaf (2003); Zeshan (2004); Savolainen (2006); The University of Jyväskylä (2018)
Flemish Sign Language	VGT	Van Herreweghe and Vermeerbergen (2006)
Hong Kong Sign Language	HKSL	Sze (2000); Tang (2006)
Indo-Pakistani Sign Language	IPSL	Zeshan (2003); Aboh et al. (2005); Zeshan (2006c)
Israeli Sign Language	ISL	Meir (2004)
Italian Sign Language	LIS	Celo (1996); Geraci et al. (2015); Branchini and Mantovan (2020)
Japanese Sign Language	NS	Zeshan (2004); Morgan (2006)
Kenian Sign Language	KSL	Akach (1991)
Mexican Sign Language	LSM	Cruz Aldrete (2008)
New Zealand Sign Language	NZSL	Zeshan (2004); McKee (2006); McKee et al. (2011)
Norwegian Sign Language	NTS	Tegnspråksutvalget (1988); Vogt-Svendsen (1990)
Quebec Sign Language	LSQ	Dubuisson et al. (1991); Bouchard and Dubuisson (1995)
Russian Sign Language	RSL	Kimmelman (2018)
Sign Language of the Netherlands	NGT	Coerts (1990); Coerts (1992); Klomp (2021)
Spanish Sign Language	LSE	Fernández Soneira (2008); Herrero Blanco (2009)
Taiwan Sign Language	TSL	Chen (2012); Tsay et al. (2015)
Trinidad and Tobago Sign Language	TTSL	Bisnath (2021)
Turkish Sign Language	TİD	Zeshan (2006b); Göksel and Kelepir (2013); Dikyuva et al. (2017)
Ugandan Sign Language	UgSL	Lutalo-Kiingi (2014)

Table 4: Sign language sample.

Author Index

Association for Computational Linguistics
209 N. Eighth Street
Stroudsburg, Pennsylvania 18360

ISBN 978-1-7138-9053-9

9 781713 890539

CURRAN ASSOCIATES INC.
proceedings.com